D1523131

English Conversation Practices

English Conversation Practices

An Intensive Course in English Supplement

English Language Institute

Maxine Guin Phinney
with
Ruth Hok
Shirley Minkewitz
Don L. F. Nilsen

Ann Arbor The University of Michigan Press

Second printing 1972
Copyright © by The University of Michigan 1968
All rights reserved
ISBN 0-472-08306-6
Library of Congress Catalog Card No. 68-29260
Published in the United States of America by
The University of Michigan Press
and simultaneously in Don Mills, Canada,
by Longman Canada Limited
Manufactured in the United States of America

Preface

THE PURPOSE of these exercises is to provide practice that approximates free conversation leading to control of common English sentence patterns. They are, therefore, intended for high-intermediate and advanced classes in English as a foreign language, or, specifically, for those students who have learned the basic patterns of statements, questions, and requests, and the following forms to be manipulated within these basic patterns:

a. Plural inflection for nouns, and the uses of *the* and *a*.
b. Present and past of regular verbs, and of common irregular verbs; progressive verb phrases; *going to* future; and negation.
c. Word order of modifiers for substantives (single words and phrases).
d. Pronouns, limiting adjectives, and question words.
e. Polite forms and *let's* for the request patterns.
f. Adverbial expressions of manner, place, and time.

The material here is intended to help the student bridge the gap between the strictly controlled drills of the training stage and spontaneous facility in the use of the newly acquired language habits. The exercises are meant to encourage the student to express his own ideas with the patterns of the new language and to change his point of view gradually from "What is it that the teacher wants me to say?" to "What would I like to say?"

The language teacher's dilemma is to balance the goal of freedom of expression with the necessity to constrain the student who is still in the process of learning. The solution for this dilemma lies chiefly in the judgment of the teacher and in the skillful use he makes of the exercises in the book. The teacher is urged, therefore, to vary the exercises according to the abilities and interests of his students and to treat the text not as a series of "exercises to be done" but rather as a source of material and ideas for lessons in English conversation.

The teacher knows what the native language of the individual student is, what his intellectual capacity and personality traits are, what his educational background is and therefore on what subject he would most likely be motivated to express himself and what standard of performance should be applied. These are all matters of judgment centered around the individual student. The textbook writers, on the other hand, can work only with impersonal factors of means and averages and optimum situations. They can at best compile exercises in graded form for specified language problems suitable for the "usual" student.

The minute the textbook enters the picture, there is the danger that the day's lesson may degenerate into the task of "doing the exercise," a task quite incongruous with a label such as "Conversation." Given proper materials, a good purpose may still be served even if this task-centered attitude prevails. But it is the ambition of those who worked on this volume that it may serve a broader purpose than merely the drilling of language habits. Whatever success is attained depends on the teacher's judgment and skill.

Those who are interested in the history of the English Language Institute materials will want to know that the bulk of what is presented here came from the unpublished "Teacher's Manual for Pattern Practice" by Maxine Guin Phinney, which carries the date 1954. Over the years this material was revised and reworked by a number of people. The final revision is the work of Ruth Hok, Shirley Minkewitz and Don L. F. Nilsen. In addition, Daniel Glicksberg, Alleen Nilsen, Maurine Nolan, Joe Palmer, Pinhkham Uparavarn, and Virginia Williams either made valuable suggestions or tested the materials in their classrooms.

Factual information used in the lessons was gathered from general source books such as *The World Almanac and Book of Facts*, *The Encyclopaedia Britannica*, and *The World Book Encyclopedia*. The anecdotes are commonly known jokes and stories retold in language suitable for our purposes here.

Harold V. King
Ann Arbor, Michigan

Suggestions for the Teacher

This volume should be considered an exercise "source book." Items are to be chosen appropriate to the student's interest and need. Consequently, the amount of time spent on individual items should vary in direct proportion to the degree of interest aroused in the class. There is an abundance of situations; it should not be necessary to linger on any that fail to bring forth spirited response. The teacher, as he plans the day's lesson, should feel free to omit what he knows will be unfamiliar, or conversely, to add suitable items on subjects of topical interest.

The teacher should not open this book with the intention of "following the script" word for word. Success in providing English conversation practice by means of the material presented here depends on the teacher's ability to tailor it into a challenge to the individual student to express himself through the various sentence patterns he is in the process of learning. Naturally, the more of them he knows, the more choice he has. This will explain why the examples given for the beginning exercises seem more controlled than those suggested for the later ones. It follows that in the later lessons the teacher will be called upon more frequently to judge whether the student's utterance is acceptable not only from the structural point of view but from the point of view of what a speaker of English would be most likely to say in a conversational setting.

Entering into this judgment obviously will be the teaching necessity of requiring use of the "new" structure even though a native speaker might just as naturally have used one from an earlier lesson which the teacher deems has been sufficiently practiced. For example, a laconic native speaker might simply answer "Yes" in a situation where a more elaborate answer would be just as appropriate. The teacher, then, with a bow to pedagogical necessity, will insist on the latter, in spite of the acceptability of the former.

In seeking to encourage the use of a variety of possible patterns, the teacher will also find that judicious prompting may be called for in order to combat the tendency to use automatically the pattern set by a previous student.

This material will be most successful in a relaxed atmosphere. The teacher should be able to start class participation smoothly and with a minimum of instruction simply by relying on the examples to set the pattern. Examples and contexts must be given slowly and with frequent pauses. The students should always feel free to ask questions. To maintain interest at a maximum it is suggested that the teacher pause after reading the cue or situation and before calling on an individual so that all those in the classroom may be encouraged to think of a response. Individual recitation should then be called for in random order.

It sometimes requires a little time and patience to initiate and maintain the give and take, but once under way it then becomes the teacher's task to balance the participation of the more articulate students with that of the more reticent ones.

The teacher should confine himself to utterances of a conversational flavor. The more experienced he is, the more adept he will be at eliciting a desired grammatical construction by the careful wording of a question, or of a rejoinder in conversational vein, without recourse to technical terminology and drawn-out explanations of classroom procedure. Grammatical terms given in the lesson titles are for the convenience of the teacher and should not necessarily be brought to the attention of the students.

Each exercise consists of four parts: (1) A brief heading states what the exercise deals with. (2) An explanation of the exercise is given to the student. Occasionally special instructions or hints to the teacher are also worked into these explanations. It will usually be best for the teacher to give these explanations orally so that the students will not become accustomed to relying heavily on their books. (3) Examples are then given to illustrate how the exercise is to be presented and to show some of the grammatical variations to be anticipated in the answer. (4) In the body of the exercise, the teacher is to choose those items best suited to stimulate the interest and imagination of the students. Some may appeal to their sense of humor; all are intended to encourage lively participation. Wherever possible, the teacher should add or substitute items which are more closely related to the students in the class. They will be much more involved in a conversation about people they all know, about places on their own campus, or about activities which they have recently participated in.

Each lesson is organized around one central idea; however, there is also a cumulative effect. The lessons are planned so that material practiced in a previous lesson will be reviewed in the following lessons without being specifically brought to the attention of the students. The lessons have not been prepared with a particular time period in mind. Some of them are longer than others, and it is to be expected that a class will sometimes cover only part of a lesson in a normal period, while on other days more than one lesson might be done.

There has been no attempt to limit the vocabulary used in the lessons. Because of the wide range of subject matters, the lessons will be suitable in classes where the students are fluent with a large vocabulary but are still in need of practice in using English grammatical structures. For those who do not have command over a great number of words, it should not be overlooked, of course, that lexical items are best learned in context and that the learning of a grammar construction and its vocabulary is something of a reciprocal process; i.e., the one helps teach the other. Therefore, if a vocabulary problem presents itself in the classroom, the teacher has three choices: he can pass quickly to another item in the exercise; or he can paraphrase the word in English; or, the others failing, he can give a quick native language translation. Asking the class to do the paraphrasing can serve to guide the conversation. Caution, of course, should be used in resorting to translation. If too frequently used, it breaks down the momentum of the class and before long the students' native language has taken over as the medium of communication.

Whatever the solution, the teacher should always keep in mind that the purpose of the exercises is not to test the factual knowledge of the student but to afford him a motive and a challenge to speak English.

The anecdotes and passages of factual information that appear in many of the lessons are intended to be presented orally in class by the teacher. The italicized items are not to be given any special stress or intonation. The italicizing is intended as an aid for the teacher in drawing the classroom activity around the indicated grammatical constructions. To emphasize them in the oral reading would only defeat the purpose of providing opportunity for unconscious use of them. Although the book is written in a style directed to the student, the teacher should present most of the material orally. If a student can comprehend the lesson without referring to the book, then the lesson will be more valuable to him because he will be forced to rely on those skills necessary in actual conversation.

A scheme of prompters on the blackboard will be found useful in exercises where responses illustrating a particular grammar point are to be chosen from among several possibilities. Such a blackboard list serves as a silent reminder for the student and makes it unnecessary to use grammatical terminology in eliciting responses. At the same time the list serves as an attention pointer making the student aware of possibilities he may otherwise overlook.

These lessons assume previous presentation and controlled practice of the underlying grammar. Even the advanced students who "know" the grammatical patterns being drilled often have difficulty in using them fluently. For this reason, we suggest that the day's work begin with more strictly controlled drills of the pattern practice type. Subsequent student performance in conversation work will thus be facilitated. In other words, the learning process proceeds from presentation of the grammar, through progressively less conscious practice, to automatic control—in that order. The last stage is gradually achieved by greater and greater attention to the thought content, as required in this volume. But to prepare for it, the students should go through the grammar and pattern practice drills first.

These lessons lend themselves to a variety of uses. They were originally intended as lessons for a teachers' manual designed to supplement the regular classroom work with a greater variety of activities, providing classroom exercises different from those assigned for laboratory or homework. In their later stages, however, they have been used as textbooks put in the hands of the students.

There is no doubt that oral presentation of the lesson material will help the student increase his aural comprehension ability. If the material is reserved as a teacher's manual, this purpose will be served automatically. Under other circumstances, it is recommended that the students' first contact with each new lesson should be through listening without looking at the book.

Many of the anecdotes and passages of factual information are suitable for giving students practice in note-taking. A follow-up exercise may be to assign a report, either oral or written, based on the notes. If this assignment is based on an anecdote, the result will be a re-telling of the story.

Dictation exercises provide another variation of activity. A dictation may be easily corrected immediately (with all the attendant benefits of such a procedure) if one of the students writes the dictation at the blackboard while the others are writing at their seats.

Much of the material of this book can profitably be adapted to laboratory work provided that the student participates by writing something or recording in some fashion in order to permit the checking of individual performance.

An opportunity for role-playing also is provided in several of the lessons, where a situation is built up to encourage highly original responses from the students. Student performance is not always predictable, for there is not just one correct response to the exercise items.

In short, as far as oral work is concerned, the teacher should always keep in mind that the goal is conversation in the English language. The subject matter is of central importance and the suggested grammar patterns are simply a device to ensure correctness of form in the utterances used. To this end then, the teacher must remember that his tone of voice and the things he himself talks about play decisive roles.

Contents

Lesson One

MODALS

Exercise 1. Use of *can, could, shall, should, might, may, must, will, would:*

The teacher will describe a situation. Use your imagination and make at least two statements about it. Each statement should include one of the words we are practicing: *can, could, shall, should, might, may, must, will,* or *would.* If the teacher writes these words on the blackboard, it will be easier to produce a variety of responses.

Examples:

Teacher: A small boy is climbing a tall tree.
Student: He should be careful. He might fall. He might break an arm or a leg.

Teacher: Tom lost his wallet.
Student: He might find it in his room. He can't go home now. He may have to borrow some money from a friend.

a. A woman is lost in a strange city.
b. John wants the family car today. It is Thursday and his father often uses the car on Thursdays.
c. Mr. Lane is driving his car fifty miles an hour in a residential area.
d. You are eating dinner with friends when the telephone rings.
e. You see an elderly woman crossing a slippery street.
f. You are in the United States. You don't know English very well.
g. Some visitors at a museum are looking for a famous picture. They see the guard.
h. Jim is at the seashore, but he doesn't swim very well.
i. Mrs. Jackson lives alone. She is very ill.
j. You are buying a car. You don't have a driver's license.
k. You are sending a package home. It contains presents for your family.

Exercise 2. Questions with modals:

The teacher will name a general subject. Make up a question using *can, could, shall, should, might, may, must, will,* or *would.* Another student answers with a short answer and a statement. Sometimes it will be possible for the answer also to include one of the modals.

Examples:

Teacher: Ask your neighbor something about mathematicians and geometry.
Student A: Can mathematicians understand the principles of geometry?
Student B: Yes, they can. They understand and use them.

Teacher: Ask about the kind of weather we are going to have tomorrow.
Student A: Will it rain tomorrow?
Student B: No, I don't think so. It probably won't rain, but it might snow.

ASK ABOUT:

a. most citizens and taxes
b. drivers and traffic laws
c. children and their parents
d. a trip around the world in a jet plane
e. the weather next winter
f. students practicing English
g. birds that sing
h. criminals and prison
i. Picasso and pictures
j. a dentist and a bad tooth
k. a broken arm and a doctor
l. a friend and a favor
m. an examination and a good grade
n. people and good manners
o. travelers and passports
p. flowers without water
q. poor eyesight and glasses
r. eight hours sleep and good health

Exercise 3. Modals in context:

Listen carefully as the teacher reads the following essay, or perhaps your teacher will want you to read along with him. Or he might read it a second time so that you can take notes. At the end he will ask you to tell about certain things using the words you have been studying. In the essay, the verb clusters using these words are italicized.

POSTAL INFORMATION

People *should know* many important things about the United States Postal Service. The Post Office divides the mail into four classes. First class mail includes sealed letters and post cards. When this essay was written, we *could send* first class mail for six cents an ounce in a sealed envelope. We *could send* post cards for five cents each. However the cost *may have risen* by now. We *may seal* all first class mail except, of course, post cards. They *can*not *be sealed.* We *must pay* ten cents an ounce for airmail to destinations in the United States. We *must* usually *pay* more for airmail to foreign countries, but we *can send* mail to Canada and Mexico at United States rates.

Second class mail includes newspapers, magazines, and other periodicals. We *can send* it for five cents for the first two ounces and one cent for each additional ounce. We *must* not *seal* this mail. It *can*not *weigh* over thirty pounds.

Third class mail is principally for advertising materials, circulars and so forth. It *may weigh* up to sixteen ounces. We *must pay* six cents for the first two ounces and two cents for each additional ounce. It *can be sealed,* but on the outside of the envelope the sender *must write* "Third Class Mail."

We have a special name for fourth class mail. It is Parcel Post. It includes merchandise, books, printed matter, and all other mailable matter not in first, second, or third class mail. Parcel Post packages *may* not *weigh* over thirty pounds if they are going a long distance to a first class post office. But if they are going to a smaller post office, they *can weigh* up to seventy pounds. The Post Office *will* not *take* packages over a certain size. We *can send* our big, heavy packages by Railway Express. For Parcel Post, we *will be charged* according to how far the package *must travel.*

The Post Office has a special category of fourth class mail: Educational Materials. It includes books, films, printed music, printed objective test materials, and manuscripts for books, periodicals, and music. We *can send* these things for twelve cents for the first pound and six cents for each additional pound. We *must mark* the package with the words "Educational Materials." We *can*not *include* personal materials such as class notes or outlines. We *should* not *seal* the package.

The Post Office *will* also *insure* and *register* mail. This is for extra safety. You *should ask* at the Post Office window about the fee.

We *can*not *send* firearms or inflammable articles by mail.

We *should* always *write* or *print* the address clearly on our letters. It is good to put a return address on all mail, but it is not necessary except on fourth class mail. There *must be* a return address on all fourth class mail.

The Postal Service is constantly trying to improve service. One recent innovation is the use of ZIP Code numbers. If a person *can remember* to put the ZIP Code on his mail, it *will* probably *be delivered* faster.

The teacher will state a subject and then call on you to tell something about it. Your statement should include one of the modals: *can, could, shall, should, might, may, must, will, would.* Information from the essay can be used, or material may be improvised.

Examples:

Teacher: sealed envelopes
Student A: Sealed envelopes must be sent with a six cent stamp.
Student B: We can send sealed envelopes to Canada for the same cost as to New York.
Student C: A sealed envelope should not be opened until it is delivered.

Teacher: first class mail
Student A: I should send personal letters as first class mail.
Student B: First class mail must be the most expensive.
Student C: First class mail will be returned if it cannot be properly delivered.

a. post cards
b. airmail to foreign countries
c. mail to Canada and Mexico
d. second class mail
e. advertising materials
f. Parcel Post
g. 30 pounds
h. Railway Express
i. educational materials
j. firearms
k. a return address
l. the Post Office window
m. ZIP Code numbers

Lesson Two

CONNECTED STATEMENTS: *Either, Too, But*

One way to understand the differences in these three words is to think of them in relationship to the following diagram which the teacher can draw on the board. First the blackboard should be divided in half with one side labeled *negative* and the other side labeled *positive*. We will list different things under each side. We will start by putting *John* and *James* on the positive side. Whenever we talk about them we will speak positively and we will use *too*. We will put *Peter* and *Paul* on the negative side and when we talk about them we will speak negatively and we will use *either*.

positive-*too*	negative-*either*
John and *James*	*Peter* and *Paul*

Examples with *too:*

John is my cousin; James is too.
John is a member of this class; James is too.
John was an apostle in the Bible; James was too.
Students continue with two or three additional examples.

Examples with *either:*

Peter was not in his room; Paul wasn't either.
Peter didn't bring his lunch; Paul didn't either.
Peter didn't get a ticket; Paul didn't either.
Students continue with two or three additional examples.

If we were to use one of the names on the positive side along with one of the names on the negative side, then we would have to use *but*. To show this, the teacher could write *but* across the dividing line.

Examples with *but:*

John is my cousin, but Paul isn't.
James isn't always on time, but Peter is.
James stumbled on the curb, but Paul didn't.
Students continue with two or three additional examples.

Exercise 1. Choosing *either* or *too:*

The teacher will add more names to the chart on the board so that it looks like this:

positive-*too*				negative-*either*		
Detroit and *Cleveland*	*Bach* and *Beethoven*	*John* and *James*	*but*	*Peter* and *Paul*	*Shakespeare* and *Cervantes*	*California* and *Michigan*

The teacher will make a statement using one of the words on the chart. Then he will point to another word and ask you a question. You are to repeat the statement and add the answer to the question using *either* or *too:*

Examples:

Teacher: (Pointing to the names): John studies. What about James?
Student: John studies and James does too.

Teacher: Peter isn't working. What about Paul?
Student: Peter isn't working and Paul isn't either.

Teacher: Bach was a musician. What about Shakespeare?
Student: Bach was a musician, but Shakespeare wasn't.

a. Shakespeare wasn't a musician. What about Cervantes?
b. Peter doesn't know much English. What about Paul?
c. John is a man. What about James?
d. California isn't in France. What about Michigan?
e. California is a state. What about Detroit?
f. Detroit is a city. What about Cleveland?
g. Bach wrote music. What about Cervantes?
h. Bach was a musician. What about Beethoven?
i. John can speak Spanish. What about Paul?
j. John might be a great engineer. What about James?

Exercise 2. Positive statements:

The teacher will name two persons, places, or things. He will also give a hint about something they have in common. Make up a sentence using the words and *too.*

Examples:

Teacher: A Cadillac and a Mercedes-Benz (expensive)
Student: A Cadillac is expensive, and a Mercedes-Benz is too.

Teacher: Shakespeare and Cervantes (great writers)
Student: Shakespeare was a great writer, and Cervantes was too.

a. roses and lilies (flowers)
b. Bach and Wagner (musicians)
c. Costa Rica and Panama (small countries)
d. Toronto and Montreal (cities in Canada)
e. Louis Pasteur and Madame Curie (famous scientists)
f. Cleopatra and Napoleon (unusual rulers)
g. Rembrandt and Rubens (artists)
h. carrots and cabbages (vegetables)
i. foxes and wolves (good hunters)
j. babies and mice (small)

Exercise 3. Negative statements:

The teacher will name the same items he gave in the last exercise, but this time he will give a negative hint about something they have in common, so when you compose a sentence, use *either*.

Examples:

Teacher: A Cadillac and a Mercedes-Benz (cheap)
Student: A Cadillac isn't cheap, and a Mercedes-Benz isn't either.

Teacher: Shakespeare and Cervantes (wrote symphonies)
Student: Shakespeare didn't write symphonies, and Cervantes didn't either.

a. roses and lilies (vegetables)
b. Bach and Wagner (scientists)
c. Costa Rica and Panama (large countries)
d. Toronto and Montreal (cities in the United States)
e. Louis Pasteur and Madame Curie (wrote poems)
f. Cleopatra and Napoleon (living now)
g. Rembrandt and Rubens (knew about penicillin)
h. carrots and cabbages (flowers)
i. foxes and wolves (eat vegetables)
j. babies and mice (strong)

Exercise 4. Choosing *either* or *too:*

The teacher will name two different items, but this time he will not give a hint about them. Make up a sentence. If it is a positive sentence use *too.* If it is a negative sentence use *either.*

Examples:

Teacher: Football and tennis

Student: Football is a sport, and tennis is too.
or: Football isn't a dance, and tennis isn't either.

Teacher: Beethoven and Chopin
Student: Beethoven wasn't a poet, and Chopin wasn't either.
or: Beethoven is dead, and Chopin is too.

a. New Mexico and New Hampshire
b. Yuri Gagarin and John Glenn
c. potatoes and carrots
d. Saturday and Sunday
e. Winston Churchill and Harold Macmillan
f. roses and violets
g. a Cadillac and a Mercedes-Benz
h. Korea and Vietnam
i. French and Spanish
j. Columbus and Magellan
k. Leonardo da Vinci and Michelangelo
l. an elephant and a tiger
m. a balloon and a lollipop
n. San Francisco and Chicago
o. squirrels and rabbits
p. London and Paris
q. buses and trains
r. Steinbeck and Hemingway

Exercise 5. Statements with *but:*

This time the teacher will make a statement about one thing and ask a question about something else. If the statement given is positive, the answer to the question should be negative. If the statement is negative, the answer to the question should be positive. The constructions should be joined with *but.*

Examples:

Teacher: He hurt his knee. What about his elbow?
Student: He hurt his knee, but he didn't hurt his elbow.

Teacher: The suit didn't come clean. What about the sweater?
Student: The suit didn't come clean, but the sweater did.

a. Kelvin was invited to the party. What about Karen?
b. The President's speech was televised. What about his opponent's?
c. My daffodils haven't come up yet. What about my neighbor's?
d. The meat is done. What about the potatoes?
e. The desk was scratched. What about the chair?

f. The maid forgot to lock the front door. What about the back door?
g. It didn't snow last night. What about rain?
h. The passengers weren't hurt in the accident. What about the car?

Exercise 6. Summary of *either, too, but*

The teacher will again make a statement and ask a question. In answering, you must decide whether to use *either, too,* or *but.*

Examples:

Teacher: Detroit isn't a state. What about Chicago?
Student: Detroit isn't a state, and Chicago isn't either.

Teacher: Magellan sailed the oceans. What about Dante?
Student: Magellan sailed the oceans, but Dante didn't.

Teacher: Shakespeare wrote long ago. What about Cervantes?
Student: Shakespeare wrote long ago, and Cervantes did too.

Teacher: He didn't get a haircut. What about a shave?
Student: He didn't get a haircut, but he got a shave.

a. Bach was a musician. What about Beethoven?
b. Marco Polo went to China. What about Julius Caesar?
c. Columbus was an explorer. What about an astronaut?
d. Tokyo isn't in Europe. What about Bombay?
e. Cleopatra didn't travel to America. What about Marie Antoinette?
f. A robin has wings. What about an elephant?
g. Abraham Lincoln was President of the United States. What about Einstein?
h. Red is a color. What about blue?
i. Steve is on the football team. What about Jim?
j. Women aren't very strong. What about children?
k. Texas is a state. What about Detroit?
l. Copper isn't a fruit. What about iron?
m. Monkeys live in Africa. What about tigers?
n. Frenchmen serve wine. What about Italians?
o. Most people don't go to school on Saturday. What about Sunday?
p. Tigers eat other animals. What about cats?
q. American men don't wear dresses. What about boys?

Lesson Three

QUESTIONS WITH *How* AND *Why*

Exercise 1. Questions with *why:*

Change the teacher's statement into a *why* question. Ask your neighbor the question so that he can give one reason behind the teacher's statement. The answer should include *in order to* or *for.*

Examples:

Teacher: You traveled a great distance to the United States.
Student A: Why did you travel a great distance to the United States?
Student B: In order to study English.
or: For schooling.

Teacher: Every city has a police force.
Student A: Why does every city have a police force?
Student B: In order to protect its citizens.
or: For the protection of its citizens.

a. Children should drink milk.
b. Children must go to school.
c. Columbus started on a long voyage in 1492.
d. People need calcium.
e. American cities provide public schools.
f. People should visit the dentist regularly.
g. Many Englishmen carry umbrellas.
h. All of the states have traffic laws.
i. Foreign students from all over the world come to the United States.
j. Some blind people walk with dogs.
k. Dairies in many countries pasteurize their milk.
l. Some pioneers in the early history of the United States went west.
m. You should know the Post Office regulations.
n. Space scientists are planning a trip to the moon.
o. Little boys need a lot of soap.
p. People should read the newspapers regularly.
q. Many students go to the movies every week.

The exercise might be repeated, this time using the shorter, less formal pattern deleting *in order.*

Examples:

Student A: Why did you travel a great distance to the United States?
Student B: To study English.

Student A: Why does every city have a police force?
Student B: To protect its citizens.

Exercise 2. Questions with *how:*

This time change the teacher's statement into a *how* question. Ask the question so that it can be answered with a pattern using *by* and an *-ing* verb form. Since there can be many answers to most of the questions, several students may answer. Notice that the negative form, *by not,* can also be used.

Examples:

Teacher: We can avoid automobile accidents.
Student A: How can we avoid accidents?
Student B: By driving carefully.
Student C: By paying attention.
Student D: By not speeding.

Teacher: Children learn from members of their families.
Student A: How do children learn from members of their families?
Student B: By watching them.
Student C: By listening to them.
Student D: By working with them.
Student E: By playing with them.
Student F: By imitating them.
Student G: By obeying them.
Student H: By not disobeying them.

a. Cities serve their residents.
b. Movie stars entertain us.
c. Television programs can educate us.
d. Everyone can learn a foreign language.
e. Mothers help their children.
f. Animals protect their young.
g. Symphony orchestras entertain large audiences.
h. Louis Pasteur helped humanity.
i. John Glenn got into the news.
j. Many men improve their living standards.

Exercise 3. Transportation questions with *how:*

The teacher will name either a person or a group of persons. Ask how these people travel or traveled. One person might give several answers beginning with *by*. The exercise as worked out here is for means of transportation, but it may be repeated to practice other types of answers, such as manner adverbials.

Examples:

Teacher: Tourists
Student A: How do tourists travel from New York to London?
Student B: They can travel by plane, or by ship. By luxury liner. By jet.

Teacher: Columbus
Student A: How did Columbus travel from Spain to the New World?
Student B: By ship. By sailing westward.

Note: Substitute or add people and places in your locale.

a. students from the campus to shopping centers
b. students from Ann Arbor to Detroit
c. people in the Sahara Desert
d. teachers to classes
e. some of the people in India
f. Charles Lindbergh
g. cowboys
h. long-distance runners
i. early American Indians
j. pioneers in the United States
k. salesmen in Detroit
l. people in this city
m. people in your city

Exercise 4. Instrument questions with *how:*

Change the teacher's statement to a *how* question so that another student can tell what equipment or instrument is used in the activity. The answers should contain *with* or *without.*

Examples:

Teacher: We are cutting tough meat.
Student A: How can we cut tough meat?
Student B: With a sharp knife. We can't cut tough meat without a sharp knife.

Teacher: We are going to measure some cloth.
Student A: How do we measure cloth?
Student B: With a tape measure. We can't do it without that or a yardstick.

Teacher: I drew circles on the blackboard a few minutes ago.

Student A: How did the teacher draw circles on the blackboard?
Student B: With a piece of chalk.

a. Engineers always measure angles carefully.
b. My sister's child, Susie, cut out paper dolls last night.
c. I should file my nails.
d. Carpenters saw wood.
e. We are going to clean the blackboard after class.
f. We record our speech in the laboratory.
g. The postman can weigh this book for me.
h. I can open a can of beans for lunch tomorrow.
i. Housekeepers sweep dirt.
j. Tourists always take a lot of pictures.
k. We usually lock our doors at night.

Exercise 5. Summary of *how* and *why* questions:

When the teacher makes a statement, convert it into a *how* or *why* question. Another student will answer using the correct grammatical construction called for by the question. Try to use a variety of patterns.

Examples:
Teacher: I mend my clothes.
Student A: How do you mend your clothes?
Student B: With needle and thread.
or: By taking them to the tailor.

Student A: Why should you mend your clothes?
Student B: To please my mother.
or: In order to look neat.

a. Cowboys travel on the range.
b. Columbus came to America in 1492.
c. Eve tempted Adam.
d. Many students go to Paris.
e. Movies usually entertain us.
f. We read the newspapers every day.
g. We are improving our English rapidly.
h. The secretaries in the office write lots of letters every day.
i. We can increase our vocabulary quickly.
j. We are going home.
k. She is washing the table.

Lesson Four

TWO-WORD VERBS

Exercise 1. Two-word verbs used in sentences:

There are certain verbs in English which are used with particles. These combinations are often called two-word verbs. The two words together have a special meaning when they are used as a unit. For example, the sentence *I called up my cousin* means that you called your cousin on the telephone, but the sentence *I called up the mountain,* probably means that you stood at the foot of a mountain and called to someone who was on the mountain. In the second sentence, *up* is not a part of a two-word verb; it merely gives direction or location.

The teacher will name some common two-word verbs and some noun phrases which might be used with them. Compose a sentence using the words.

Examples:
Teacher: look for—passport
Student: I am looking for my passport.

Teacher: set aside—work
Student: She set aside her work when I came.

a. turn off—radio
b. try on—shirt
c. hand in—test
d. talk over—problem
e. take over—country
f. call up—friend
g. check out—book
h. read over—composition
i. keep at—lessons
j. think over—proposal
k. hope for—letter
l. ask for—date

Exercise 2. Separable two-word verbs:

One of the interesting things about two-word verbs is that they do not always occur together. Sometimes, but not always, they can be separated by a noun phrase. The following sentences which the teacher will read use verbs of this kind. They are called separable. The noun phrase used with the two-word verbs can either come between the two words or can follow them. The teacher will say the sentence with the noun phrase following the two words. Repeat each sentence, only change it so that the noun phrase separates the two-word verbs.

Examples:

Teacher: Whose turn is it to *clear off* the table?
Student: Whose turn is it to *clear* the table *off?*

Teacher: She forgot to *wind up* the clock.
Student: She forgot to *wind* the clock *up.*

a. It will only take a minute to *brush off* the lint.
b. Would it be all right if I *tried on* this coat?
c. Reluctantly the young mother *gave up* her baby.
d. The director *bawled out* Mr. Winters.
e. Every night he *cleans out* the pool.
f. Please *turn off* the TV.
g. I'm going to try to *get back* my book.
h. On Tuesday you must *hand in* your report.
i. Especially in forests you should be careful to *put out* your cigarette.
j. You'll probably feel better after you *talk over* the problem.

Exercise 3. Separable two-word verbs used with pronouns:

One of the things which causes difficulties for speakers using two-word verbs is that when they are used with a pronoun in place of the noun phrase, they have certain restrictions. Sometimes the pronoun must be inserted between the two parts of the verb, while at other times it must follow the two parts. For example if the sentences in Exercise 2 were changed to use pronouns, the pronouns would have to be inserted between the two parts of the verb because these were separable two-word verbs. The teacher will repeat the sentences from Exercise 2 putting the noun phrase within the two-word verb. Repeat the sentence, only change the noun phrase to a pronoun.

Examples:

Teacher: Whose turn is it to *clear* the table *off?*
Student: Whose turn is it to *clear* it *off?*

Teacher: She forgot to *wind* the clock *up.*
Student: She forgot to *wind* it *up.*

a. It will only take a minute to *brush* the lint *off.*
b. Would it be all right if I *tried* this coat *on?*
c. Reluctantly the young mother *gave* her baby *up.*
d. The director *bawled* Mr. Winters *out.*
e. Every night he *cleans* the pool *out.*

f. Please *turn* the TV *off.*
g. I'm going to try to *get* my book *back.*
h. On Tuesday you must *hand* your report *in.*
i. Especially in forests you should be careful to *put* your cigarette *out.*
j. You'll probably feel better after you *talk* the problem *over.*

Exercise 4. More separable two-word verbs:

This time the teacher will say sentences which he wants you to repeat, again changing the noun phrase to a pronoun and putting it between the two parts of the verb. It will be a little harder because the teacher's sentences do not all have the two-word verbs separated. However they are all verbs which can be separated so when you use them with a pronoun, you must put it between the two parts of the verb.

Examples:
Teacher: Let's try to *scrape off* the old paint first.
Student: Let's try to *scrape* it *off* first.

Teacher: You can *rinse* your shirt *out* in the hotel room.
Student: You can *rinse* it *out* in the hotel room.

a. Help! I can't *turn off* the water!
b. How soon will they have *made up* the schedule?
c. I *have* Tuesday *off.*
d. We're responsible for *putting on* the program.
e. Let's hurry and *finish up* this project.
f. Police were looking for the driver who *ran down* the pedestrian.
g. The recipe said to *fold in* the egg yolks.
h. It didn't take the new president long to *take over* the company.
i. The criminals reluctantly *gave up* the money.
j. He *turned over* the deed to the new owners.
k. You mustn't *wind up* your watch too tightly.
l. She didn't feel like *dressing* her children *up* for the party.
m. Aunt Mary *brought* her children *up* on a farm.
n. It's very hard to *wake up* thirty-six Boy Scouts every morning.

Exercise 5. Non-separable two-word verbs:

There are other two-word verbs which cannot be separated by a pronoun. If a pronoun is used it must follow both parts of the verb. Even when a noun phrase is used, it too must follow the complete verb. If your feel for English is well enough developed you might test out one or two of these sentences to see if the noun phrase could come between the two parts of the verb. For instance, it is perfectly appropriate to say "His socks don't *go with* his tie," but it would sound very strange to say *"His socks don't *go* his tie *with*." Although there is no rule to follow and no way to know for sure except to ask a native speaker, you can probably get some feel for non-separable two-word verbs by practicing with the ones in the following sentences. When the teacher reads a sentence change it so that you are using a pronoun in place of the noun phrase. Be sure that the pronoun follows the two-word verb.

Examples:

Teacher: He *called on* the student.
Student: He *called on* him. (Not *He *called* him *on*.)

Teacher: I'll *call for* Sandra tonight at 9:00.
Student: I'll *call for* her tonight at 9:00.

a. Angie *insisted on* having a big church wedding.
b. We *called on* Miss Tidwell.
c. She's been *going with* Tom since December.
d. His mother said we could *depend on* Jack.
e. I think it was the first time she had ever *waited on* the manager.
f. The chocolate cake *tastes like* mint.
g. I always felt that he was *laughing at* his wife.
h. He *looks like* his grandfather.
i. I go to the zoo to *laugh at* the monkeys.
j. He doesn't know how to *get down to* business.
k. I wouldn't *dream of* cheating.
l. It takes several weeks to really *get over* pneumonia.

Exercise 6. Distinguishing separable and non-separable two-word verbs:

The teacher will read a sentence using a two-word verb with a noun phrase. Change the sentence so that the noun phrase is a pronoun. Where possible insert it between the parts of the verb. If it is a non-separable two-word verb, be sure to place the pronoun after the complete verb.

Examples:

Teacher: *Call up* Jane.
Student: *Call* her *up*.

Note: It would be incorrect to say *"*Call up* her."

Teacher: I'm *hoping for* a letter in today's mail.
Student: I'm *hoping for* it in today's mail.

Note: It would be incorrect to say *"I'm *hoping* it *for* in today's mail."

a. Did you *pay for* the watch?
b. Let's *call on* Aunt Mary.
c. Don't *insist on* overtime pay.
d. May I *try on* the dress?
e. She *checked out* the book yesterday.
f. I need to *rinse out* my sweater.
g. I will *drive away* my new car this afternoon.
h. Let's *talk about* a party.
i. She *set down* the groceries.
j. She *turned over* the class to a new teacher.
k. John *drove by* the new house.
l. Please *read over* my composition.
m. The truck *ran over* my bicycle.
n. He didn't *put out* the campfire.
o. Did you *subscribe to* "The Daily"?
p. Sally is *waiting for* Dick.
q. The salesgirl didn't *wait on* Janet.

Exercise 7. Pronouns used with separable and non-separable two-word verbs:

Now the teacher will say a sentence which has two parts. In the second part a two-word verb will be used. The noun phrase used with it is the same as the one used in the first part of the sentence. Change it to a pronoun so that the style of the sentence will be much better. Again, you will have to distinguish whether or not you are using a separable two-word verb.

Example:

Teacher: Someone really made a mess here; I wonder who will *clean up* the mess.
Student: Someone really made a mess here; I wonder who will *clean* it *up*.

Teacher: He had the flu, but he *got over* the flu.
Student: He had the flu, but he *got over* it.

a. Old friends attend class reunions; *running into* old friends is most of the fun.
b. The traffic is very bad; I wonder what's *holding up* the traffic.
c. Susan seems very happy, but I think John is just *leading* Susan *on*.
d. I'm not sure that it's going to rain, but it *looks like* rain.

e. When you have finished with the books, *drop* the books *by* my house.
f. He's excited about the new proposal, but I'm not sure he can *put over* the new proposal.
g. My dress doesn't fit well; I think I should *take in* my dress around the waist.
h. If you have measles when you are young, you can usually *get over* the measles easier.

Exercise 8. Two-word verbs in context:

As your teacher reads this story, notice the two-word verbs in it. Afterwards you will talk about the story.

A DOG MISBEHAVES

Mrs. Sam Powell went with her husband to an important conference in a large city. She and her husband *checked into* a very nice hotel where her husband's company was *putting up* all its employees. Mrs. Powell remembered that her old school friend, Mrs. Stanley, lived in that town. "I might *call on* her. We can *talk over* old times. I'll *look* her *up* in the telephone directory," she thought.

The first day at the hotel, Mrs. Powell had planned to write letters, but she *set* them *aside* and *called up* her friend. Mrs. Stanley was delighted. She was planning to go shopping, but she said she would *put* it *off* until later. She *insisted on* having Mrs. Powell *drop by* that very afternoon.

A taxi *picked up* Mrs. Powell in front of her hotel. It took a long time to get to Mrs. Stanley's because an accident was *holding up* the traffic. At last the driver *pointed out* a large and beautiful house with very impressive gardens. Mrs. Powell quickly *put out* her cigarette. She wished she had *dressed up* more. She wished that she had *kept on* her fur coat and that she had *put on* gloves and a hat.

As she walked up the long path to the house, a huge dog came bounding around a corner and nearly *ran over* her. "It *looks like* a lion," she thought. She was afraid, but she walked towards the house bravely. A servant opened the door, and the dog ran in beside Mrs. Powell. It ran madly around the room and jumped up on the lovely furniture. At first Mrs. Powell wondered if she should *laugh at* the dog's tricks. But then as she *listened to* a loud crash caused by a falling lamp, she began to *wish for* something to appease the dog with. She really didn't *approve of* having dogs as house pets. She *made up* her mind that she would certainly *think* it *over* before she got a dog.

Mrs. Powell wondered if the dog were trying to *show off,* or if perhaps it were a joke that she didn't *catch onto.* "He certainly shouldn't be allowed to *get away* with this behavior," she thought. He was actually *taking over* the living room. Mrs. Stanley called her servant. Mrs. Powell could tell that she was quite *put out* at the dog's behavior. She was sure that Mrs. Stanley was going to *give up* and have the dog put outside, but instead Mrs. Stanley calmly asked the servant to *straighten up* the room and then to *bring in* something for the dog to eat.

The servant brought in some food which *consisted of* sirloin steak and raw eggs. The dog quickly *gobbled up* the food and *barked for* more. Again the servant *brought in* fresh meat and the dog *ate* it *up,* this time spilling some on the carpet. When the dog looked up hungrily, the servant apologized saying that he had *run out* of fresh meat.

Mrs. Powell couldn't *get over* this kind of behavior. She felt very embarrassed and began *looking for* an excuse to leave. At four-thirty, she said "I must go now. My husband will be *waiting for* me." Her dear old school friend said goodbye coolly. At the door she asked, "Are you going to leave your dog here?" Mrs. Powell *looked at* her friend in amazement. "My dog! It isn't my dog!"

As a class, re-tell the story. Here are some clues which might help you. Your teacher will read the clues and then ask you to make a statement about that part of the story. After you have done this, perhaps one or two of you can tell the story without any prompting. It might be a good idea to write "Mrs. Powell, the visitor," and "Mrs. Stanley, the hostess," on the board. In some of your telling, you will undoubtedly use two-word verbs, but do not consciously try to use them in every sentence.

a. with her husband
b. a nice hotel
c. her husband's company
d. old school friend
e. call on her
f. old times
g. telephone directory
h. planned to write letters
i. planning to go shopping
j. that very afternoon
k. a taxi
l. took a long time
m. a large and beautiful house
n. Mrs. Powell wished
o. a huge dog

p. a servant opened the door
q. laugh at the dog's tricks
r. something to appease the dog with
s. dogs as house pets
t. if perhaps it were a joke
u. called her servant
v. she was quite put out
w. calmly asked the servant
x. brought in some food
y. the servant apologized
z. she felt very embarrassed
aa. my husband
bb. said goodbye coolly
cc. leave your dog
dd. at her friend in amazement

Lesson Five

INFINITIVES

Exercise 1. Use of a verb + *to* + verb:

Some of the verbs in English which are commonly used with *to* plus another verb are *decide, learn, intend, plan, need, like, try, hope, expect, promise, want,* and *have.* The teacher will give a clue from the story "A Dog Misbehaves." You should ask a question using the teacher's clue and one of the verbs listed above. When a class member answers he should also practice the pattern by using one of the above verbs with *to.*

Examples:

Teacher: look up an old friend
Student A: Did Mrs. Powell want to look up an old friend?
Student B: Yes, she did. She wanted to look up an old college friend.

or

Student A: Who did Mrs. Powell plan to look up?
Student B: She planned to look up her old friend, Mrs. Stanley.

or

Student A: Why did Mrs. Powell decide to look up an old friend?
Student B: She decided to look up an old friend in order to talk over old times.

Teacher: put out the dog
Student A: Did Mrs. Stanley try to put out the dog?
Student B: No, she didn't. Mrs. Stanley tried to quiet the dog.

or

Student A: When did Mrs. Stanley try to put out the dog?
Student B: She didn't. She wanted Mrs. Powell and her dog to feel at home.

a. talk over old times
b. look her up
c. call up her friend
d. call on Mrs. Stanley that afternoon
e. ran up to her
f. look like a lion

g. eat up the meat
h. run out of dog food
i. take it out of here
j. get along with it
k. look at her friend

Exercise 2. Practice with *intend, plan, need, like, try, hope, expect, promise,* and *want:*

Make a series of statements telling what your parents wanted you to do. Try to use the words listed above.

Examples:

Student A: My parents wanted me to study engineering. They planned for me to go to school. They expect me to study hard.
Student B: I wanted to be a doctor. I like to help people. My parents needed me to work at home, but they finally promised to let me study medicine.
Continue with each student

Exercise 3. Questions with *learn, intend, plan, need, like, try, hope, expect, promise, want,* and *have:*

The teacher will make a statement. Change the teacher's statement to a question using one of the above words. Another student should answer the question, also using the word.

Examples:

Teacher: A doctor helps people.
Student A: Does a doctor want to help people?
Student B: Yes, he wants to. He wants to help them.

Teacher: People often ask doctors to help them.
Student A: Do people need to ask doctors to help them?
Student B: Yes, they often need to ask doctors to help them.

Teacher: Carlos is speaking English.
Student A: When did Carlos learn to speak English?
Student B: He learned to speak English last year.

Teacher: Mathematicians sometimes make mistakes.
Student A: Do mathematicians try to make mistakes?
Student B: No, they try not to.

a. Mothers care for their children
b. Most teachers instruct their students patiently.
c. Police arrest careless drivers.
d. Husbands take care of their wives.
e. Columbus sailed for India.

f. Early settlers in California found gold.
g. We are speaking English.
h. Space scientists make trips to the moon.
i. A lazy person leaves the work to other people.
j. Citizens pay taxes in most countries.
k. Many prisoners escape from prison.
l. Careful drivers sometimes have accidents.
m. Dentists hurt their patients.
n. A careful janitor leaves a dirty floor.
o. A good wife always pleases her husband.

Exercise 4. Verbs + *to* in context:

Listen carefully as the teacher reads this story so that at the end you can re-tell parts of it. The verb clusters with *to* are italicized.

A FAMOUS MUSICIAN

George Frederick Handel was a German musician. He lived in the eighteenth century. His father *wanted him to be* a lawyer. George *wanted to become* a musician. His family *tried to discourage* his enthusiasm for music. His father *told him not to talk* about it. He *wouldn't allow George to have* any kind of musical instrument.

George was very *anxious to learn to play* the clavichord. (A clavichord is an early version of the modern piano.) An uncle in another city *didn't want George to be unhappy*. He brought a small clavichord to the Handel home. He and George hid it in the attic. George practiced there at night. He *was not afraid to go up* to the attic alone.

George couldn't practice every night because it bothered his older brother who often *wanted to stay up* late and read. But the clavichord was *easy for George to learn to play*. He could play it very well within a few months.

One night his father discovered him. We can see the scene in a famous picture. Little George is sitting at the clavichord in the attic. He is wearing his night clothes and a little sleeping cap. The picture shows his father at the door with a lamp in his hand.

His father was very angry. He *ordered the servants to take* the clavichord away. George *had to promise his father not to practice* again.

George was *old enough to leave home* a few years later. He went to another city. He *asked a famous duke to listen* to his music. The duke *permitted George to play* several of his original compositions. He was very complimentary: The music was brilliant. After this success, George's father *allowed him to study* music. He *continued to write and perform* all of his life. You probably know his very famous composition, "The Messiah."

What do you remember about this famous musician? See if you can tell something about him or about the story we just read. Use the teacher's hint in your sentence.

Example:
Teacher: a lawyer
Student: George's father wanted him to be a lawyer.

a. a musician
b. his enthusiasm for music
c. not to talk about it
d. any kind of a musical instrument
e. his uncle
f. the clavichord
g. the attic
h. his older brother
i. one night George's father
j. ordered the servants
k. George had to promise
l. George was old enough
m. he asked a famous duke
n. the duke permitted
o. after this success

Lesson Six

DESCRIBING RELATED FACTS

Exercise 1. Positions of *very, too, enough:*

The teacher will state some related facts. Listen to them and then ask a question which will lead your classmates to a conclusion about the facts. The questions and answers should include *very, too,* or *enough.*

Examples:

Teacher:	The shoes are size 10. Jim wears size 9.
Student A:	Are the shoes too large for Jim?
Student B:	Yes, they are too large for Jim to wear.
Teacher:	The typewriter weighs fifteen pounds. Mary wants to carry it to school.
Student A:	Is the typewriter light enough?
Student B:	Yes, it's light enough for Mary to carry to school.
Teacher:	The soup is boiling. John is in a hurry. He's hungry.
Student A:	Is the soup very hot?
Student B:	Yes, it is very hot. John will have to wait to eat it.

a. John is twenty-one. He wants to drive a car.
b. The wooden bridge is old. The truck weighs two tons.
c. Betty has a high fever. She wants to go to a picnic today.
d. The man is ninety years old. He wants to play tennis.
e. Susan has a 1931 Ford. Her boyfriend wants to use it for a trip to Chicago.
f. My sweater is black with dirt. Fred wants to wear it.
g. The chocolate is bitter. The baby wants some.
h. The big cowboy hat belongs to Uncle Bill. His little nephew asked to wear it to school.
i. Mrs. Bright bought a new dress. When she washed it in hot water it shrunk.
j. Mr. and Mrs. Chandler bought a big old farmhouse. They have six children. They need a lot of room to live in.

Exercise 2. Use of such adjectives as *easy, difficult, complicated, heavy, hard, far, small, expensive,* etc. in *for + noun and to + verb* pattern

The teacher will make a statement which you are to ask a question about using one of the adjectives listed above. If you are called on to answer a question, try to use a sentence pattern which includes *for* + a noun or noun substitute and the infinitive *to* + verb which you practiced in Lesson Five.

You might also want to use *too, very,* or *enough.*

Examples:

Teacher: The machine weighs a hundred and fifty pounds.
Student A: Is the machine heavy?
Student B: Yes, it's heavy for a woman to carry.
or: Yes, it's too heavy for a woman to carry.

Teacher: The problem involves algebraic equations.
Student A: Is the problem difficult?
Student B: Yes, it's difficult for me to solve.
or: Yes, it's very difficult for me to solve.

a. The lesson has two hundred pages.
b. The distance is three thousand miles.
c. The house has twenty rooms.
d. The car is a Volkswagen.
e. The teacher speaks rapidly.
f. The fruit is sweet.
g. The chair isn't comfortable.
h. Exercises are sometimes complicated.
i. The problem isn't easy to solve.
j. The suit is very nice looking.
k. The apartment has only two rooms.
l. Her vacuum cleaner weighs 23 pounds.

Lesson Seven

EXPLETIVES

Exercise 1. It in subject position:

This is a completion game. The more unusual the completions, the more fun it will be. The teacher will begin the game with an introductory clause containing *it* in subject position. The first student adds a *for* phrase, and the third student finishes with a *to* phrase.

Examples:

Teacher: It was difficult.
Student A: It was difficult for him.
Student B: It was difficult for him to paint a picture.

Teacher: It is necessary.
Student A: It is necessary for the teacher.
Student B: It is necessary for the teacher to assign homework.

a. It isn't easy.
b. It was quite impossible.
c. It was unusual.
d. It was difficult.
e. It's convenient.
f. It's interesting.
g. It's really fun.
h. It isn't hard.
i. It was extremely difficult.
j. It's going to be easy.
k. It should be convenient.
l. It would be nice.

Exercise 2. There in subject position:

The teacher will tell something about a particular situation. Then he will state a conclusion which an observer could have come to. See what kind of detectives you are by asking questions which would lead to the teacher's conclusion. In your questions use the phrases *is there, are there, was there* and *were there*. All the questions for a particular case may be directed to an individual student who answers them either in the affirmative or the negative.

Examples:

Teacher: You enter a dining room. Eight people will soon be eating dinner.

Student A: Are there eight napkins on the table?
Student B: Yes, there are eight napkins on the table.
Student C: Are there eight forks on the table?
Student B: Yes, there are eight forks on the table.
Student D: Are there only five chairs at the table?
Student B: No, there aren't. There are eight chairs at the table., etc.

a. You saw a bad accident on your way home yesterday. Someone was hurt.
b. You enter a large living room for the first time. You decide: "This is a professor's home. He has a baby daughter."
c. John entered a room. He decided: "This is a classroom but it must be a holiday."
d. Mary went to a baseball game with her boyfriend yesterday. The winning team was his favorite.
e. All of the students went to a movie last Saturday. It was a western.
f. You saw a big fire. A private home was burning.
g. Your classmates are riding on a bus. They are going to a picnic at the beach.

Exercise 3. It in subject position as an answer to a question:

Briefly describe a situation and then ask a question about it so that another student can answer your question with *it* in subject position. Answers of this kind usually deal with such things as time, weather, distance, identification of person, existence of qualities, etc. In asking the questions, many different grammatical constructions can be used.

Examples:

Student A: Everyone eats turkey. What day is it?
Student B: It's Thanksgiving.

Student A: We are eating lunch. What time is it?
Student B: It's twelve-thirty. (or: It's noon.)

Student A: I'm going to Washington, D.C. tomorrow. How far away is it?
Student B: It's five hundred miles.
or: It's a long way.

Student A: I wore a heavy coat and boots to school today. What kind of weather is it?
Student B: It's cold weather.

Student A: There is a strange noise at the door. What is it?
Student B: Maybe it's a child.
or: Perhaps it's the custodian.

Continue.

Lesson Eight

POSSESSIVES

Exercise 1. Distribution of the *of* and the *'s* patterns:

This exercise will give you practice in producing the *'s* to show possession. When we talk about inanimate objects, it is common to use the *of* pattern but when we talk about people or animals we usually use *'s*. After you have practiced this exercise, you might do it again, inserting adjectives.

Examples:

Teacher: Tell me something about a machine and its work.
Student: The work of a machine is usually beneficial to man.
or: A machine's work is usually beneficial to man.

Teacher: Tell me about a teacher and his responsibility.
Student: A teacher's responsibility is to teach.

a. Tell me something about the President and his latest news.
Channel 2 and its news program.

Note: of sometimes means *about*, so it is better in this set to use *'s*, because "News of the President," might be interpreted as "News about the President" rather than news that he is reporting.

b. Tell me something about the Republican party and its public relations.
the University and its public relations.
a manufacturing company and its public relations.
a politician and his public relations.

c. Tell me something about a special committee and its report.
the report your friend wrote for class.
a professor and his report.

d. Tell me something about a political party and its newspaper.
your city and its newspaper.
New York and its many newspapers.

e. Tell me something about the class and its progress.
Mary and her progress.
the medical profession and its progress against cancer.

Exercise 2. *'s* used with periods of time:

A common English usage is to speak of something as if it belonged to a certain period of time. The teacher will name something. Make up a sentence about it, changing the time period to _____ *'s.*

Examples:
Teacher: a meeting held this morning
Student: This morning's meeting was very enjoyable.

Teacher: a storm last month
Student: Last month's storm caused heavy damage to farms.

a. some news announced today
b. a class that is graduating this year
c. a report of things happening this month
d. the paycheck you will receive this week
e. a dance held last Saturday
f. a reception given last night
g. a study made during this year
h. a snow storm that came yesterday
i. the newspaper issued on Monday
j. the rain that fell last winter
k. a heat wave last summer
l. an airline strike last spring
m. the *Life* magazine coming out next week
n. fog that was in the air yesterday morning
o. a vacation next month
p. fashions worn next season

Exercise 3. Use of *whose, mine, yours, John's, his, hers,* etc.

Look around the classroom and describe something you see. Ask whose it is. Your teacher might call on one person to answer, or he might have the whole class answer together.

Examples:
Student A: I see a blue necktie. Whose is it?
Student B: It's John's
or: (indicating a person) It's his.

Student B: There's a heavy red book on the desk. It isn't mine. Whose is it?
Student C: It's the teacher's.

Student C: I need to borrow a pencil. Whose is that one?
Student D: It's mine.

Student D: Mary has my chair. Whose is that one?
Student E: It's hers.

Student E: There's a book with a green cover on the second chair from the window. Whose is it?
Student F: It's Bill's.

Student F: Fred has a gray coat, but this one isn't his. Whose is it?

Continue.

Lesson Nine

PRONOUNS

Exercise 1. The use of *who, where, when, why, what,* and *how:*

Remember the story in Lesson Five about the famous musician, George Frederick Handel? Perhaps your teacher will read it again. Then he will give you hints from the story. Use one of the question words listed above and ask a fellow student something about the story.

Examples:

Teacher: in the eighteenth century
Student A: When did Handel live?
Student B: He lived in the eighteenth century.

Teacher: a lawyer
Student A: What did his father want him to be?
Student B: His father wanted him to be a lawyer.

a. Germany
b. a musician
c. any kind of musical instrument
d. clavichord
e. an uncle
f. in the attic
g. late at night
h. his older brother
i. stay up and read
j. his father found him
k. the servants were ordered
l. George had to promise
m. a few years later
n. to another city
o. a famous duke
p. several original compositions
q. the famous "Messiah"

Exercise 2. One and *ones* as substitutes:

This is a completion exercise. Repeat what the teacher says and then add another clause pointing out something that is opposite from the subject in the first statement. Instead of repeating the subject, substitute *one* or *ones.* Watch carefully for mass nouns. If the teacher gives you a statement using a mass noun, you must repeat it in the second part of the sentence. Do not substitute *one* or *ones.*

Examples:

Teacher: This is a new building.
Student: This is a new building and that is an old one.

Teacher: A Cadillac is an expensive car.
Student: A Cadillac is an expensive car; a Volkswagen is a cheap one.

Teacher: This is good coffee.
Student: This is good coffee; that is bad coffee.

a. These are tall telephone poles.
b. I drove on a smooth highway.
c. This is a good movie.
d. I don't have much money.
e. We are good students.
f. This is cold water.
g. These are high mountains.
h. This is thick soup.
i. This is a heavy object.
j. This is blue ink.
k. This is a fast train.
l. This is an easy lesson.
m. These are pretty houses.
n. These are intelligent men.
o. He drew straight lines.
p. She always serves tender meat.

Exercise 3. *One* and *ones* in context:

Listen while the teacher reads this information about the United States. Notice the use of *one* and *ones*.

There are fifty states in the United States of America. Thirteen of these were the original states. They were the *ones* in the Union at the close of the Revolutionary war. Some of the original states were Connecticut, Delaware, Georgia, Maryland, Massachusetts, Pennsylvania, Rhode Island, South Carolina, and Virginia.

There are two recent additions. The newest *ones* are Alaska and Hawaii. Both of these entered the Union in 1959.

Texas used to be the largest state. Texans were very proud of this fact. Now Alaska is the largest *one*. It is about twice the size of Texas. The smallest *one* is Rhode Island. It measures fifty miles from border to border. The longest state used to be California, but now Alaska is the longest *one*. It is about 130 miles longer than California.

The state with the highest altitude is Alaska. The *one* with the lowest altitude is California. Mount McKinley in Alaska is more than 20,000 feet high. Death Valley in California is 282 feet below sea level.

The state with the largest population used to be New York, but now it is California. Those with the smallest populations are Alaska and Nevada. The latter has about 60,000 more people than the other *one*.

Now show what you know about the United States by using the phrases which the teacher gives you, in a sentence. Feel free to use any grammatical pattern which you would like.

Example:

Teacher: fifty states
Student: There are fifty states in the United States.

Teacher: original states
Student: The original states were the ones in existence at the close of the Revolutionary War.

a. original ones
b. recent additions
c. Alaska and Hawaii
d. in 1959
e. before 1959
f. used to be Texas
g. very proud
h. largest one
i. about twice the size
j. Rhode Island
k. border to border
l. the longest one
m. about 130 miles longer
n. the highest point
o. the lowest point
p. more than 2,000 feet
q. 282 feet below
r. the largest population
s. smallest population
t. about 60,000 more people

Exercise 4. Questions with pronouns:

Use the teacher's hints and ask some questions about the United States. Your neighbor will answer them. Use such question words as *who, where, when, why, what,* and *how.* You might also try to use *one* and *ones* in some of the questions or the answers.

Example:

Teacher: fifty states

Student A: How many states are there?
Student B: There are fifty states all together.

Teacher: thirteen
Student A: How many of the states were the original ones?
Student B: There were thirteen original ones.

a. the original ones
b. two recent additions
c. Alaska and Hawaii
d. the longest one
e. the highest point
f. the lowest point
g. more than 20,000 feet
h. 282 feet below
i. largest population
j. smallest population
k. Texas
l. the largest one
m. the smallest one

Lesson Ten

COMPARISONS

Exercise 1. Comparisons with *like, the same as,* and *different from:*

The teacher will suggest some things to be compared. Ask a question about them using such phrases as *like, different from,* and *the same as.* The student who answers will probably find it helpful to use such phrases as *just, almost, exactly, somewhat, about, more or less,* etc. Notice how the meaning changes when you stress the words.

Examples:

Teacher: a lion and a leopard
Student A: Is a lion like a leopard?
Student B: Yes, a lion is almost like a leopard, but a leopard has spots.

Teacher: a lion and an elephant
Student A: Is a lion different from an elephant?
Student B: Yes, a lion is quite different from an elephant. A lion is smaller than an elephant.

a. an orange and a grapefruit
b. a duck and a goose
c. a banana and an orange
d. a horse and a zebra
e. the product of two times four and the product of four times two
f. a one-dollar bill and a five-dollar bill
g. spring and summer
h. a mouse and a cat
i. a quarter of an hour and fifteen minutes
j. Michelangelo and Leonardo da Vinci
k. this school and one in your country
l. traffic laws in this city and those in your city
m. a wolf and a dog
n. a donkey and a horse
o. a cherry and a grape
p. Washington, D.C. and New York, N.Y.

Exercise 2. Use of *the same* ________ *as:*

The teacher will make a statement describing something in a pattern using *as* ________ *as.* Change the statement so that you are saying the same thing only using the pattern *the same* ________ *as.*

For instance, if he uses the adjective *wide*, you will use the noun *width*.

Examples:

Teacher: This pencil is as long as that one.
Student: You mean, this pencil is the same length as that one.

Teacher: My typewriter is as heavy as yours.
Student: In other words, my typewriter is the same weight as yours.

a. People in the country are, on the average, as tall as those in the city.
b. The man at this machine works as fast as the woman at that one.
c. Girls can learn as quickly as boys.
d. A lizard is sometimes as long as a snake.
e. An apple is usually as large as an orange.
f. Highways in Michigan are about as wide as those in California.
g. That peach on the table is about as heavy as an orange.
h. There are country roads in Michigan as narrow as some in Ohio.

Exercise 3. Use of *as* ________ *as:*

This time the teacher's statement will be in the noun pattern: *the same* ________ *as*. Change his noun to an adjective or an adverb and use *as* ________ *as* pattern.

Examples:

Teacher: John's pen is the same price as Paul's.
Student: You might say, John's pen is as expensive as Paul's.

Teacher: A truck doesn't go at the same speed as a car.
Student: That's true; a truck doesn't go as fast as a car.

a. A BB shot can't penetrate to the same depth as a bullet.
b. This book isn't the same size as that one.
c. Bob is the same age as Bill.
d. That fire engine is the same color as that ambulance.
e. Bob had the same number of shirts in the laundry last week as Bill.
f. Bob didn't have the same amount of money in the bank last year as Bill.
g. The Chrysler Building is not the same height as the Empire State Building.

Exercise 4. Comparisons with *-er* and *more:*

The teacher will make a statement. Ask a question based on his statement. Devise your question so that the student who answers it will be making a comparison either with *more* or *-er*.

Examples:

Teacher:	It's cold in Chicago in the winter and it can be cold in Los Angeles too.
Student A:	Is it colder in Chicago in the winter than it is in Los Angeles?
Student B:	Yes, of course. It's always colder in Chicago in the winter.
Teacher:	A lion is a dangerous animal and a dog can be too.
Student A:	Is a dog more dangerous than a lion?
Student B:	No, a dog is seldom more dangerous than a lion.

a. A car is expensive and an airplane is too.
b. Most men are courageous and most children are too.
c. Mt. Everest is high and Mt. McKinley is too.
d. It rains frequently in Florida and it sometimes snows there too.
e. An orange is sweet but a lemon isn't.
f. June is long and July is too.
g. A sunset is beautiful and a sunrise is too.
h. A rabbit runs fast and a dog does too.
i. Boys can be intelligent and girls can too.
j. Most men are strong but few women are.
k. The Ohio River is wide and the Mississippi River is too.
l. Columbus was adventuresome and Magellan was too.
m. A plane moves fast and a rocket does too.

Exercise 5. Questions with *as* ________ *as* and *the same* ______ *as:*

This time, in addition to changing the pattern of the teacher's statement as you did in Exercises 3 and 4, make it into a question. The student who answers should use *-er* or *more*.

Examples:

Teacher:	A tiger is as big as an elephant.
Student A:	Is a tiger the same size as an elephant?
Student B:	No, it's smaller than an elephant.
Teacher:	Your neighbor probably has the same amount of money as Henry Ford.
Student B:	Do you have as much money as Henry Ford?
Student C:	No, I don't. He has much more than I have.

Teacher: A kangaroo travels at the same speed as a turtle.
Student C: Does a kangaroo usually travel as slowly as a turtle?
Student D: No, a kangaroo can travel many times faster than a turtle.

a. September has the same number of days as January.
b. A camera is the same size as a transistor radio.
c. A Ford is as expensive as a Volkswagen.
d. A cherry is the same color as a strawberry.
e. Chicago is the same distance from Detroit as Cleveland is.
f. A worm is as long as a snake.
g. Spain has the same climate as California.
h. Mary weighs as much as Jane.

Exercise 6. Distribution of *-er, -est* and *the most:*

Your teacher will draw pictures on the board which will be useful in talking about such things as length, width, and size. When the teacher points to the items, you can tell him something about them. Use *the most,* or the endings *-er* and *-est.* Perhaps he will have the class speak in unison, after you are accustomed to the exercise.

Example:
Teacher: These are pieces of string.
Students: A is longer than B. A. ————————————
B is longer than C. B. ————————
C is shorter than B. C. ————
B is shorter than A.
A is the longest of the three pieces.
C is the shortest of the three pieces.

a. These are three cities, New York, Chicago, and Ann Arbor.

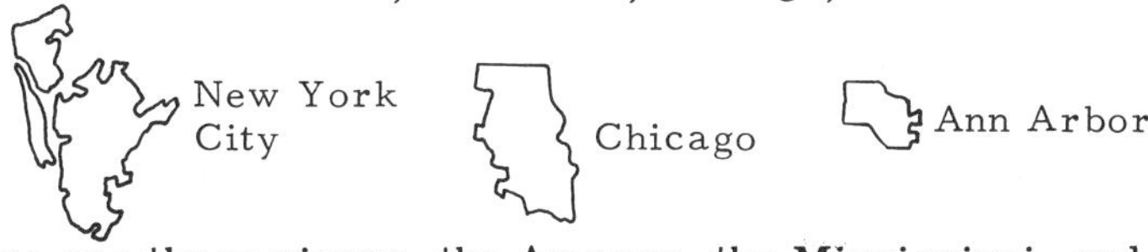

b. These are three rivers, the Amazon, the Mississippi, and the Detroit.

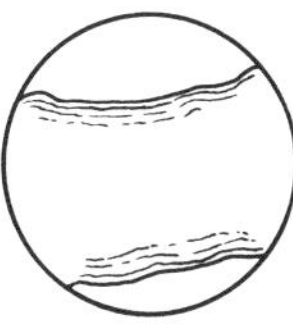
Amazon

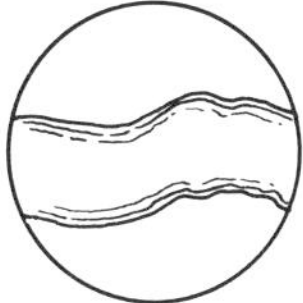
Mississippi

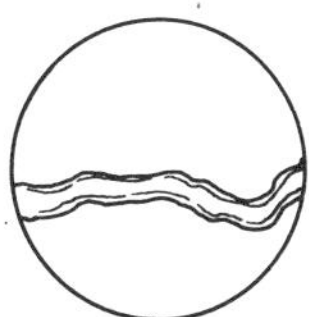
Detroit

c. These are three mountains, Everest, McKinley, and Whitney.

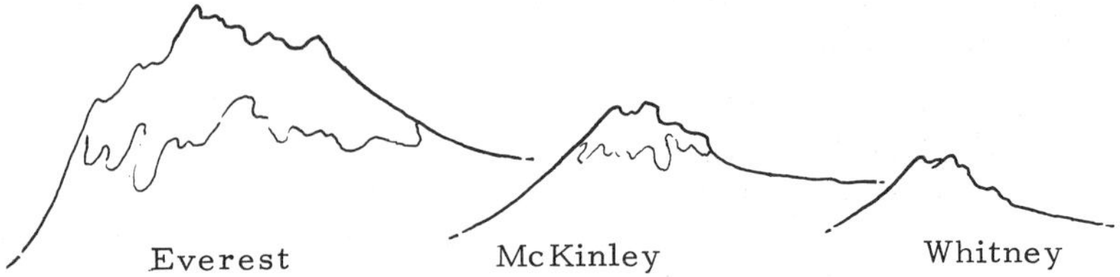

d. These are three weights, a 2,000 lb. weight, a 200 lb. weight, and a 50 lb. weight.

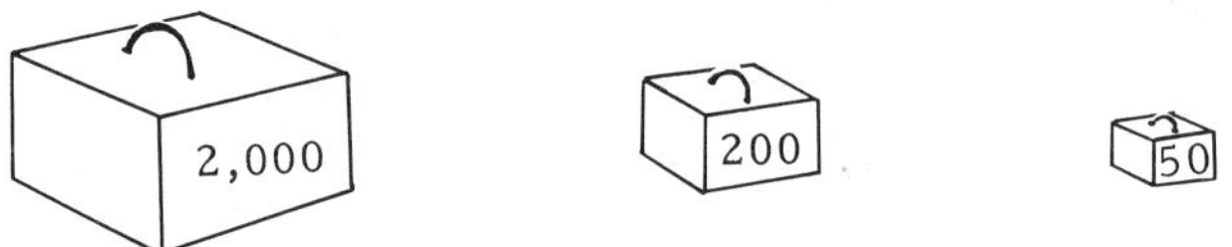

e. These are three surfaces, a gravel one, a concrete one, and a glass one (compare smooth and rough).

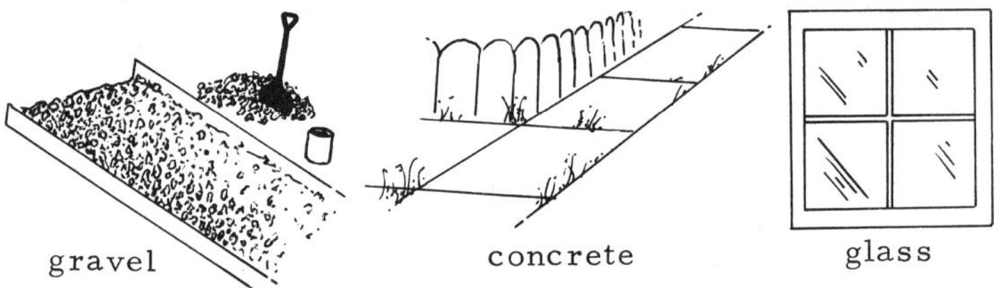

f. These are three boys, a sixteen-year-old, a ten-year-old, and a two-year old (compare heights and ages).

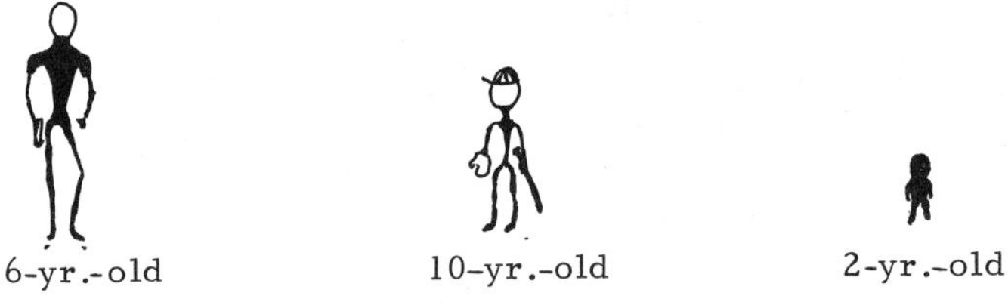

g. These are three books, a pamphlet, a pocketbook, and a desk dictionary.

Exercise 7. Spontaneous practice with comparisons:

Look at the pictures again. Ask a classmate a question about any of them. You should now be able to compare and talk about them in a random order.

Examples:

Student A: Which boy is the oldest?
Student B: The tallest boy must be the oldest.
or: The sixteen-year old is older than the others.
or: The one who is sixteen is the oldest.

Student A: Which mountain would you want to climb?
Student B: The smallest one, what about you?
Student C: I'm braver; I would choose the biggest one.

Exercise 8. More spontaneous practice:

There is a popular guessing game called "Twenty Questions." The person who is "it" thinks of an object or a person. The other players try to guess what he is thinking of. If they do not guess the right answer in twenty questions, they are the losers. When you play this game, try to formulate your answers around the comparative and superlative patterns learned in this lesson.

Examples:

Student A: I am thinking of a person.
Student B: Is he as famous as the Premier of the U.S.S.R.?
Student A: Yes, he's as famous as the Premier of the U.S.S.R.
Student C: Is he as old as the President of the U.S.?
Student A: He's older (or younger) than the President of the U.S.
Student D: Is he as important as the Prime Minister of England?
Student A: He is just as important as the Prime Minister of England.
Student E: Is he the most important official in France?
Student A: Yes, he is.
Student F: Is it . . . ?
Student A: Yes, it is.

Lesson Eleven

RELATIVE CLAUSES

Exercise 1. Use of *who* and *that* in questions and statements about people:

The teacher will name a certain occupation. Using a relative clause modifying a noun, ask a question about who that person is. The student who answers should make a complete statement so that he too gets practice in making relative clauses. *Who* is the most common way to introduce a relative clause about a person, but *that* is also used in less formal situations.

Examples:

Teacher: an author
Student A: Is an author a person who paints pictures?
Student B: No, an author is a person that writes.

Teacher: a carpenter
Student A: Is a carpenter a man who builds houses?
Student B: Yes, a carpenter is a man who works with lumber and nails.

a. a plumber
b. a doctor
c. a lawyer
d. a cowboy
e. a policeman
f. a clerk
g. a senator
h. a teacher
i. a truck driver
j. a custodian
k. an astronaut
l. an actor
m. a nurse
n. a dentist
o. a movie star
p. a printer
q. an architect

Exercise 2. Use of *that* and *which* in questions and statements about things:

When the teacher asks you a question about a tool, a supply, or a piece of equipment, answer by giving a complete statement. Use a relative clause just as you did in the last exercise, only this time you will use either *that* or *which.*

Examples:

Teacher: Is a hammer a tool which carpenters use?
Student: Yes, a hammer is a tool which pounds nails.

Teacher: Is a knife something that cuts meat?
Student: Yes, a knife is something that cuts meat and many other things too.

a. Is an iron something that presses clothes?
b. Is a ballpoint pen something that is used in a ball game?
c. Is a clip board something that holds paper or something that holds paper clips?
d. Is a dryer something that is dangerous?

Now the teacher will give you a subject and you make up the questions so that another student can answer.

a. a toothbrush
b. a comb
c. a bobby pin
d. hairspray
e. shoe polish
f. a screw driver
g. a paint brush
h. a mop
i. a broom
j. a scrub brush
k. a radio
l. a clothes brush
m. a vacuum cleaner
n. a curtain rod
o. a tractor
p. a plow
q. a shovel

Exercise 3. Use of *where* and *that* and *which* in statements about places:

This time the teacher will name a place. He will call on several of you to make a statement about the place. In your statement include a relative clause. If you are speaking of the place to show where something is, then you will use *where.* But if you are speaking of the place as a certain thing, then you will use *that* or *which.*

Examples:

Teacher: Washington, D. C.

Student A: Washington, D. C. is the place where I got lost last fall.
Student B: Washington, D. C. is the city which is the capital of the United States.
Student C: Washington, D. C. is the city that I would most like to visit.

Teacher: a bank
Student A: A bank is a place where we can cash checks.
Student B: A bank is something which must be well built.
Student C: A bank is usually a building which is clean and attractive.
Student D: A bank is a place that policemen watch carefully.

a. a supermarket
b. a drive-in theater
c. Canada
d. Paris
e. the pyramids
f. California
g. Disneyland
h. New York City
i. The Grand Canyon
j. a dining room
k. Tokyo
l. Brazil
m. a laundromat
n. a post office
o. a service station
p. Niagara Falls

Exercise 4. Use of *that, which,* and *when* in statements about time:

The teacher will name a holiday or a period of time. Make a statement about it using a relative clause. If you speak of it as a way of establishing the time of something use *when.* But if you speak of it as an event, use *which* or *that.*

Examples:
Teacher: Christmas
Student A: Christmas is a time when people feel kind.
Student B: Christmas is a holiday which is not celebrated in my country.
Student C: Christmas is something that I do not understand.

Teacher: Fall
Student A: Fall is the season which I like best.

Student B: Fall is the time of year when we go on picnics.
Student C: Fall is the time of year when airlines lower their rates.

a. Easter
b. winter
c. spring
d. July
e. New Year's
f. Thanksgiving
g. Sunday
h. five o'clock
i. eight o'clock
j. September
k. yesterday
l. tomorrow
m. next month

Exercise 5. Use of *who, that, which, when,* and *where:*

The teacher will ask questions this time. When you answer try to use the appropriate relative pronoun.

Examples:

Teacher: What country would you like to visit?
Student: Kuwait is the country that I would like to visit.

Teacher: Which movie actor impresses you most?
Student: Richard Burton is the movie actor who impresses me most.

a. What time of year do you prefer?
b. Which sport do you like to watch?
c. Which games do you like to play?
d. Who is President of the United States?
e. What is the language that you are learning to speak?
f. Who was the man who invented the telephone?
g. What is the meal that we eat in the morning?
h. Who was the man who made the first non-stop flight across the Atlantic Ocean?
i. Who is the man that is in charge of this school?
j. What is the product that miners produce?
k. What is the meat that comes from cows?
l. What is the instrument that tells us directions?
m. What is the instrument that takes pictures?
n. Who are the people who live in the White House?
o. When is it that we hide Easter eggs?
p. What is the time when we eat lunch?
q. What was the time that Cinderella had to leave the King's Ball?

Lesson Twelve

TIME EXPRESSIONS

Exercise 1. Use of *for, during, when,* and *while:*

The teacher will make a statement. Complete the statement by adding a phrase telling either how long the activity was going on, or when it happened. There could be many different things added to each of the statements. Make your phrase begin with *for, during, when,* or *while.*

Examples:

Teacher:	They studied.
Student:	They studied for two hours.
or:	They studied during the evening.
or:	They studied when they needed to.
or:	They studied while I danced.

a. We usually go to Florida.
b. The electricity went off.
c. The dog barked.
d. Mary sometimes cries.
e. My sister had to stay home.
f. Henry traveled around Europe.
g. Mary had to walk on crutches.
h. They never speak with me.
i. Mary and John went sight-seeing.
j. I should practice my English.
k. It rained.
l. The bus stopped.
m. We plan to go shopping.
n. The people shouted.

Exercise 2. Use of *for, during, when,* and *while:*

The teacher will give only part of a sentence. Think of his phrase as part of a time statement. Make up a complete sentence using that time statement. You will have to use *for, during, when,* or *while* preceding the phrase.

Examples:

Teacher: John was driving
Student: The baby slept while John was driving.

Teacher: three hours
Student: The baseball game lasted for three hours.

a. the parade began
b. the concert
c. the phone rang
d. it was raining
e. a long time
f. the afternoon
g. several hours
h. the house was burning
i. the insect stung him
j. the flight
k. it was time for the count-down
l. a little while
m. the cake was burning

Exercise 3. Use of *before, until,* and *after:*

The teacher will name a person. Tell us something about that person. In your sentence use either *before, until,* or *after.*

Example:

Teacher:	President Kennedy
Student A:	Mr. Kennedy was a senator before he became President.
Student B:	He became President of the United States after the 1960 election.
Student C:	He was President until his assassination.

a. Abraham Lincoln
b. John Glenn
c. Joan of Arc
d. William Shakespeare
e. Christopher Columbus
f. George Frederick Handel (the musician in Lesson Five)
g. Madame Curie
h. Charles Lindbergh
i. Pilgrims who are important in United States history.
j. Dwight D. Eisenhower
k. your own father
l. your favorite relative
m. a person who lives close to you
n. yourself

Exercise 4. Time expressions in context:

As the teacher reads this story, notice the time expressions. Listen carefully so that when it is finished you can retell parts of it.

SILENCE IS GOLDEN

Once upon a time there was an office worker whose name was Charles. He worked in the same insurance office *for* many years. But *during* that time, he became more and more unhappy. *While* he worked, he dreamed constantly, and in his dreams he was always a hermit. *When* he went home at night, he stayed in his room. He didn't like people. He especially didn't like people *when* they talked. He wanted peace and quiet. Life went on for Charles in this way *until* he became desperate.

His big opportunity came *when* he learned about a sea voyage that two of his friends were planning. They expected to make the trip *during* their summer vacation. Charles asked to join them. *While* they were sailing, our hero talked to his friends about the joys of a hermit's life. He talked *until* he finally convinced them and they decided to stop at the first island that they found.

A few days *after* this decision, they saw an island in the distance where they decided to live. *Before* they went ashore, Charles asked the other two to make a promise. They had to promise not to say a single word *after* they reached the island. They were to remain perfectly quiet *during* their stay.

During the first few days *after* they landed, they built a little house near which they planted a garden. The island was paradise for Charles because this was the peace and quiet that he wanted.

Everything was fine *for* a year. Then, one day, it happened. His two friends, as usual, were taking their morning walk. One man went in one direction around the little island *while* the other man went in the opposite direction. When they met on the beach, one man said to the other, "It's lovely here, isn't it?" Then each man continued on his way.

After another year, the two met again on the beach. "Yes, it is," was the reply. One morning *after* still another year, Charles woke up very angry.

"There is too much talk on this island," he shouted.

Now retell the story. The teacher will give you some clues to help. When it is appropriate use *for*, *during*, *when*, *while*, *before*, *until*, and *after*. Perhaps the teacher will write these words on the board to help you use them.

a. the same insurance office
b. more and more unhappy
c. he dreamed constantly
d. home at night
e. he especially didn't like
f. he became desperate
g. a sea voyage that two of his friends were planning
h. their summer vacation

i. they were sailing
j. he convinced them
k. the first island
l. this decision
m. make a decision
n. a single word
o. a little house
p. a garden
q. paradise
r. the opposite direction
s. they met on the beach
t. very angry

Now answer the teacher's questions about "Silence is Golden." Again try to use the words which we are studying.

a. How long did Charles work in the same office?
b. When did he become unhappy?
c. When did he dream?
d. What did he do at night?
e. What was it that he didn't like?
f. How long did Charles continue in this manner?
g. When did his big opportunity come?
h. When did his friends plan to make their trip?
i. When did Charles talk to his friends about the joys of a hermit's life?
j. Was Charles persistent?
k. When did they see the island?
l. When did Charles ask his friends to make the promise?
m. What was the promise?
n. How long did they have to keep the promise?
o. When did they build the little house?
p. When did they plant the garden?
q. What were the first words that the friends spoke after they arrived on the island?
r. How long did the man have to wait for the answer?
s. When did this conversation take place?
t. How much time passed before Charles became angry?
u. How long were they on the island before Charles spoke?

Lesson Thirteen

Wh- CLAUSES FUNCTIONING AS DIRECT OBJECTS

Exercise 1. *Who, what, when, which,* and *how* clauses in object position:

The teacher will ask a question with *who, when, what,* or *how.* Repeat the question, but introduce it with a phrase such as *do you know, can you tell me, do you remember,* etc. Sometimes you will have to adjust the word order accordingly. Ask another student the question. If he knows the answer he gives it; if not, he says so and asks the class for the answer. He should make a complete sentence repeating the pattern of the question. In this way, both of you will get practice with the usual question word order, and you will also see what grammar adjustment is necessary when one of these words which you are studying is placed in object position.

If you are asked a question and you do not know the answer, merely ask someone else. The important thing for you to do is to practice English, not to memorize facts. It is just as important to learn to answer questions negatively as positively. If no one in the class knows the answer, then a statement should be made to that effect. It can be in the same sentence pattern.

Notice how the questions sound more conversational when *you* is stressed.

Examples:

Teacher: Who invented the telephone?
Student A: Do you know who invented the telephone?
Student B: Yes, I know who it was. It was Alexander Graham Bell.
or: No, I don't know who it was. Who can tell us who invented the telephone?
Student X: I can tell you who it was. It was Alexander Graham Bell.
or: No one in our class knows who invented the telephone.

Teacher: Who was Marconi?
Student A: Do you remember who Marconi was?
Student B: Yes, I remember who he was. He invented the radio telegraph.
or: No, I can't remember who he was. Does anyone remember who Marconi was?
Student X: I remember who he was. He was the inventor of the radio telegraph.

a. Who was Marilyn Monroe?
b. Who are the New York Yankees?
c. When did Columbus discover America?
d. Who invented the incandescent light bulb?
e. What did Ernest Hemingway do?
f. Who was Huckleberry Finn?
g. How many hours are there in a day?
h. What does Frank Sinatra do to entertain his audience?
i. Who painted the "Mona Lisa"?
j. How many hours are there in a day?
k. How far is it across the English Channel?
l. What did Robert Frost write?
m. How often is there a full moon in the calendar that the Americans use?
n. What was the name of one of John Steinbeck's famous books?
o. When is Thanksgiving?
p. How often is Leap Year?
q. When is the next exam going to be?
r. When did the man in the chair by the door arrive in the United States?

Exercise 2. Converting statements to questions with *who, what, when, which,* and *how* clauses in object position:

This time the teacher will make a statement. Change it into a question using *who, what, when, which,* or *how.* Again you will need to use the phrases *do you know, can you tell me,* and *do you remember.* Answers should be given in the same manner as in Exercise 1.

Examples:

Teacher: She discovered radium.
Student A: Do you know who discovered radium?
Student B: Yes, I know who discovered it. It was Madame Curie.

Teacher: The United States Independence Day is in July.
Student A: Can you tell me when the United States Indepencence Day is?
Student B: Yes, I can tell you when it is. It's July 4.

a. This man helped the boy get a clavichord in the story about the famous musician, George Frederick Handel.
b. This month is the shortest of the year.
c. This is the largest state of the United States.
d. This man was the first President of the United States.
e. This season has the warmest weather of the year.
f. This book belongs to somebody.

g. This tool cuts wood.
h. This mountain is the highest in the world.
i. This fruit has a yellow peel.
j. This color is a combination of blue and yellow.
k. This country is the largest in South America.
l. This month has the fewest days.
m. This meat comes from pigs.
n. This object helps us clean our fingernails.

Exercise 3. Guided practice:

Think of an important person to ask another student about. Or look at the objects around the room and ask questions about them. Your questions and answers should follow the same patterns as those in the preceding exercises.

Lesson Fourteen

That CLAUSES FUNCTIONING AS DIRECT OBJECTS

Exercise 1. Use of *that* + sentence (about a person) in direct object position:

Another pattern which could be used to answer the questions in Lesson Thirteen is one using *that* to introduce a sentence which is functioning as a direct object. As you will see, this pattern takes fewer words. In the first part of this exercise the teacher will name an occupation. In the second part he will name a famous person. Compose the same kind of questions as you did in the last lesson, using the phrases *can you tell me, do you remember,* and *do you know.*

The student who answers should use such phrases as *I know that, I believe that, I suppose that, I imagine that, I think that, I guess that, I remember that,* and *it seems that.* Perhaps your teacher will place these phrases on the board to encourage you to use them all. When you do not know an answer, you might say *I guess that, I imagine that,* or *I don't think that . . . .* Even when an American speaker is sure of an answer he often uses a phrase such as *I think* or *I believe* so that he sounds less firm and unyielding. He doesn't think of their literal meaning.

Examples for first part:

Teacher: A jeweler.
Student A: Do you know what a jeweler does?
Student B: I know that he repairs watches.

Teacher: An usher.
Student A: Do you know what an usher does?
Student B: I believe that he shows people to their seats at the theater.

a. a banker
b. a butcher
c. a detective
d. a postman
e. a maid
f. a real estate agent
g. a chemist
h. a contractor
i. a beautician
j. a clerk

Examples for second part:

Teacher: Shakespeare
Student A: Do you know what Shakespeare did?
Student B: I know that he wrote great dramas.

Teacher: Sir Isaac Newton
Student A: Do you remember what Sir Isaac Newton did?
Student B: I believe that he formulated the law of gravity.

a. Winston Churchill
b. Napoleon
c. Caesar
d. Columbus
e. Cleopatra
f. Copernicus
g. Santa Claus
h. Sir Edmund Hillary
i. Nero

Exercise 2. Use of *that* + sentence (about a thing) in direct object position:

This exercise is the same as the last one, except that you will not be talking about people.

Example:

Teacher: a rabbit.
Student A: What do you know about a rabbit?
or: What can you tell me about a rabbit?
Student B: I know that it's a small animal and that it likes carrots.

a. a hammer
b. a watermelon
c. a camera
d. a turnip
e. a ball park
f. the tango
g. a saxophone
h. a donkey
i. spaghetti
j. a ruler
k. a typewriter
l. a duck

Exercise 3. Deletion of *that* in *that* + sentence construction:

This time the teacher will ask the questions. When you answer use the same construction as you did in the last two exercises, only this time delete *that*. This deletion of *that* is very common, especially in conversation. It does not change the meaning. However, if the sentence is a rather involved one, *that* is usually retained so that the pattern is made clearer. Perhaps your teacher will want you to answer the questions both ways.

Examples:

Teacher: Is Sunday the first or last day on the American businessman's calendar?
Student: I believe it is the first day.

Teacher: Who is John Glenn? Was he the first or second American to orbit the earth?
Student: I think he was the first American astronaut to orbit the earth.

a. Does a Cadillac cost more or less than a Mercedes-Benz?
b. What is the population of Tokyo?
c. What is a French poodle? What kind of people usually own a poodle?
d. Is baseball like a game in your country?
e. Do they speak Spanish or Portuguese in Brazil?
f. On which continent do we find the Sahara Desert?
g. Where does Picasso (or some other famous person) live today?
h. Does everyone in the class like to eat cookies?
i. Would you be able to climb the highest mountain in the world?
j. Which city in Michigan is called "The Motor City"?
k. Do you think that you will ever visit the smallest state in the United States.
l. Do you know anyone who has pearls that came from oysters?
m. Could you teach me to dance "Swan Lake"?
n. What do people use oil for?
o. Do we all have metal desks at home?
p. When does Santa Claus visit the homes of American children?
q. Do you know what a philatelist is?

Exercise 4. That + sentence constructions in context:

As the teacher reads the following essay on colleges and universities in the United States, listen carefully and even take notes on some of the facts, or perhaps the teacher will want you to read along with him. In addition he will ask you to tell what you remember about the colleges. In discussing this material, you will probably find it natural to use the *that* + sentence pattern which you have been practicing. In addition, you will get a chance to use the other relative clauses as well as some of the time expressions which you have studied in the last few lessons.

COLLEGES AND UNIVERSITIES OF THE UNITED STATES

In 1636, a short time after the first colonists came to the territory which we now call Massachusetts, the General Court of Massachusetts made the first appropriation for Harvard College. Most of you have probably guessed *that this school is the one that later became the famous Harvard University.* It is the oldest university in the United States. Not many people know *that it was named in honor of John Harvard,* who died in 1638. This man left his library and half of his property to the new institution.

After the establishment of Harvard, wealthy people as well as religious leaders who believed *that the future of the new country depended on education,* began to establish other schools. By 1776, which was the year that Americans declared their independence, nine other institutions were in operation. Their present names and the dates of their establishment are:

College of William and Mary (1693)
Yale University (1701)
Princeton University (1746)
Washington and Lee University (1749)
Columbia University (1754)
University of Pennsylvania (1755)
Brown University (1764)
Rutgers College (1766)
Dartmouth College (1770)

Some of the money for the colonial colleges came from the colonial governments, but most of it came from people who felt *that by donating their money they were investing in the new country.* Other people also believed *that the new country needed colleges.* These people voted for their state governments to organize colleges which would be supported by taxes. These are called state universities, and they play leading roles in the world of education today. By 1894 all states south and west of Pennsylvania had such universities. The University of Michigan which first opened as a school in Detroit in 1817, became a state university in 1837, when Michigan became a state.

In the early 1800's most people thought *that only men should attend college.* However other people felt certain *that women too must be educated.* Some of them thought *that the best way would be to have co-educational colleges,* but others felt *that there should be separate colleges for men and women.* Oberlin College, which was one of the first co-educational schools, dates from 1833. Mount Holyoke, which was founded in 1837, was the first school exclusively for women. Other institutions which are especially for women are Vassar (1861), Wells (1868) and Wellesley (1871). In 1870 when Michigan, Illinois, Missouri, and California began to admit women to the state universities, some people felt *that it was not right.* However, ideas have changed and now no university that receives its support from public funds can refuse to admit women. Even many of the privately sponsored men's colleges are now beginning to admit women to their graduate programs. By this we can see *that ideas about American education are still changing.*

When answering the teacher's questions, perhaps you will use some of the phrases which you have been studying. Not all of the questions can be answered with *that* clauses. In some of them you will use the relative pronouns *who, what, when, which,* and *how;* in others you will have an opportunity to use time expressions. In this kind of a review exercise, the important thing is not for you to concentrate on a certain pattern, but for you to speak naturally. Perhaps you will be surprised at how easily you now use some of these patterns. If you do not remember an answer, simply make up a sentence saying something like "I don't remember what . . . ."

Examples:

Teacher: Now do you know where Harvard is?
Student: Yes, I know that Harvard is in Massachusetts.

Teacher: Do you remember the name of the man that Harvard College was named after?
Student: Yes, his name was John Harvard, and he was the man who donated his library and half of his property to the college.

a. Did you learn which is the oldest university in the United States?
b. Do you remember when John Harvard died?
c. Do you suppose that this is why they named the college after him?
d. What happened in 1776 that was so important to the United States?
e. Can you remember how many colleges there were at this time?
f. Why did people support the colonial colleges?
g. Can you tell me what happened in the nineteenth century to state universities?
h. What did you learn the term "state university" means?
i. Do you remember why the date 1837 is significant in the history of The University of Michigan?
j. What were some of the different ideas that early settlers had concerning the education of both men and women?
k. What do you remember about Oberlin College which dates from 1833?

l. One of the women students should remember what was said about Mount Holyoke. Do you?
m. Name some other colleges that are especially for women.
n. What kind of college cannot refuse admission to women?
o. What are some private colleges for men now beginning to do?
p. What does this show us about American education?

Now the teacher will call on various class members to describe the types of colleges and universities that we find in the United States. You might tell the class how they developed chronologically, as they were presented in this essay. Or you might choose to tell about colonial colleges while another student might tell about state universities, and another student might tell about women's colleges, etc. Or your teacher might encourage you to have a question and answer exchange with each other.

Lesson Fifteen

THE VERB *Have*

Exercise 1. The use of *have* with *just, for, since, been* + *(verb)ing,* and *(verb)ed:*

The teacher will describe something that has happened. Use your imagination and tell about the situation. Make five different statements so that you can practice *have* in each of the patterns suggested above. In some of the sentences you will probably be using more than one of the patterns. Perhaps the teacher will write a set of examples on the board for you to follow. Notice how *have* changes to *has* when speaking in the third person singular. Also notice how your sentences will sound more conversational if you use the contracted form, i.e., *I've* rather than *I have* and *she's* rather than *she has.*

Examples:

Teacher: You were downtown on a shopping trip. What do you tell your family when you come home?

Student: I've just been downtown.
I've been shopping for several hours.
I've been shopping since 10:00 this morning.
I've been looking at coats, but I didn't find one I liked.
I've wasted the morning.

Teacher: Mary is getting off the bus after a two-day trip. Use your imagination to tell us some things about Mary.

Student: She's just come back from a trip.
She hasn't slept well for two nights.
She's been sitting up since day before yesterday.
She's been trying to read.
She's traveled halfway across the United States.

a. When John stops at a drug store for a soda after a game of tennis, he often meets a friend. What might he say to him?
b. When Mr. and Mrs. Lane come home from a three-day fishing trip, what do they tell their neighbors?
c. When Bob goes to a dance he never comes home early. You meet him in the hall about 2:00 one morning. He is wearing evening clothes. What do you conclude?
d. After a long and difficult examination, what do you say to your roommate?
e. You buy a brand new car after looking for several days. What can you tell your friends?

f. Mrs. Lane wrote letters for several hours. What can you tell about Mrs. Lane?
g. Bob and Richard got back an hour ago from a long hike in the mountains. What can you tell about them?
h. Mrs. Lane gave her dog a bath one morning. The dog didn't like it. Mrs. Lane worked at it for an hour. What do you think she told her husband when he came home for lunch?

Exercise 2. The use of *have* with *finally, all day* (*night, week,* etc.), and *since* (*because*) + sentence:

This time make three statements about the situation which your teacher will describe. Use the words given above. *Finally* is used in the same way as *just* to mean that something has recently been completed.

You will probably use *been* + *(verb)ing* with the *all day* construction. When using the *since* + sentence construction, you will be using *since* in a different way than you did in the last exercise where it was an indication of time. Here it has the same meaning as *because.* If you would rather, you can use *because.*

Example:
Teacher: After you returned home from an all-night fishing trip, you telephoned a friend to tell him about it. What did you say?
Student: I've finally gotten home.
I've been fishing all night.
I haven't had any sleep because we got frightened and didn't dare stay in the tent.

a. You return home after studying in the library for several hours. You have a difficult examination tomorrow. What might you tell your roommate at dinner?
b. John has been working on his car. The car runs smoothly now. What do you know about John?
c. Bob is hiking and gets to the top of a mountain where you are waiting for him. What can you tell about Bob?
d. You and Bill finish a long conversation about life. What can you tell someone about the conversation.
e. You have painted your house. It took weeks of hard work. What can you tell your friends?
f. Mrs. Lane left the hospital after a month. What did she write to her friends?
g. You and Bill played three sets of tennis. What did you tell a friend about the game when you were having coffee afterwards?

h. John and Mary are having their dessert in a restaurant. What can you tell about the meal?

Exercise 3. Have used in questions and answers:

The teacher will make a statement to you. Pretend that you have forgotten something. Ask the class to help you remember what it is. Let them ask you questions until they guess what you've forgotten or until you remember. Use forms of *have* in the questions and answers.

Example:

Teacher: You are going to make a long trip by car.
Student A: I am always so forgetful! What have I forgotten to do?
Student B: Have you packed everything you need?
Student A: Yes, I have. I've packed everything.
Student C: Have you told your friends about the trip?
Student A: Yes, I have. I've told them all about it.
Student D: Have you asked the company to disconnect the telephone?
Student A: Yes, I've taken care of that.
Student E: Have you notified the milkman?
Student A: Yes, I have. I've told him not to leave any more milk.
Student G: Have you filled the tank with gasoline?
Student A: Yes, I have. I filled it yesterday.
Student H: Have you changed the oil?
Student A: That is what I've forgotten. I've forgotten to change the oil.
(or, if nobody is able to guess:)
Student A: I remember now. I've forgotten to put air in the tires.

a. You and some friends are going on a picnic.
b. You have an examination in English tomorrow. You hope to get a good grade.
c. Jane is getting ready for a dinner party.
d. The Lanes are getting ready for a trip abroad.
e. You are going to take your best girl to a formal dance tonight.
f. You plan to buy a new car.
g. Dr. Brown is on his way to the home of a very sick patient.
h. A fire starts in a large rooming house. The owner is a very forgetful person.

Exercise 4. Use of *had* and *hadn't:*

The teacher will make a statement about something that has already happened. Ask another student a question about it. Since you will be speaking in the past tense, you will use *had* instead of *have* or *has*. If the student doesn't know the answer, then he should ask another student. You might use words like *before* and *when* in formulating your questions.

Examples:

Teacher: Columbus started on a voyage around the world to India.
Student A: Had Columbus received permission from the rulers of Spain before he started?
Student B: I don't know. Had he?
Student C: I think that he had.

Teacher: Alaska became a state.
Student A: Had Alaska become a state before World War II?
Student B: No, it hadn't. It became a state later.

a. Louis Pasteur finished his studies at the university.
b. Marco Polo wrote about his adventures in China.
c. John Kennedy served in the U. S. Navy.
d. There was a revolution in Cuba in 1959.
e. Shakespeare wrote his first drama. (radio? television?)
f. Joan of Arc fought for France.
g. Many foreign students came to the United States after World War II.
h. Two airliners collided over New York City in 1961.
i. South Africa became a republic in 1961.
j. The (White Star Liner) Titanic struck an iceberg and sank in 1912.
k. Charles Lindbergh made a non-stop flight from New York to Paris in 1927.
l. General George Washington became President of the United States.
m. The American Revolution lasted from 1775 to 1783.

Exercise 5. Forms of *have* in context:

The teacher will read a short essay about silicosis. Notice the use of the various forms of *have* as he reads it.

SILICOSIS

Silicosis is a disease of the lungs. It is prevalent among miners who *have been working* in mines for a long time. These men *have been breathing* air which is filled with quartz particles. After a time, they often develop silicosis.

In the late 1930's, research scientists started to work on the problem. Mine owners *had understood* for many decades that the miners were afraid of silicosis. It *had been* one of the great causes of tuberculosis among miners. Of the many attempts to prevent the disease, none *had been successful* before 1938. It was then that the scientists began their experiments with fine aluminum dust. They found that aluminum dust forms a coat of protective jelly around each quartz particle in the lungs. The sharp little particles of quartz *had* usually *cut* the delicate lining of the lungs. With the coat of jelly around them, they couldn't penetrate and it was easy to exhale them.

The work with aluminum dust *has been* very effective. The miners must breathe it each day before they begin their work. Since the introduction of this method of prevention, there *have been* fewer cases of silicosis. Since silicosis *has* not *caused* so many cases of tuberculosis among the miners they *have* not *been* afraid to work.

The mine doctors *have noticed* a remarkable decrease in the numbers of silicosis patients since the first experiments. The troublesome quartz particles which *had been* so dangerous before *have caused* little trouble since.

The teacher will give a phrase from the essay. Use it in a sentence. With most of the sentences you can use a form of *have*.

Examples:

Teacher: a disease of the lungs
Student: Many miners used to have a disease of the lungs.

Teacher: it is prevalent
Student: It is most prevalent among miners who have worked for many years.

a. air which is filled with quartz particles
b. in the late 1930s
c. mine owners
d. a great cause of tuberculosis
e. many attempts to prevent silicosis
f. scientists and their experiments
g. the penetration of quartz particles in the lungs
h. quartz is easy to exhale
i. the experiments and their success
j. the miners each day
k. fewer cases of silicosis
l. the number of cases of T.B.

m. doctors have noticed
n. the troublesome quartz particles

Now the teacher will repeat the clues. This time if you are called on, make up a question using a form of *have*. The student who answers it should also use *have, had,* or *has*.

Lesson Sixteen

THE VERB *Be*

Exercise 1. Forms of *be: am, was,* used with first person:

As you probably know, *be* is a rather special verb in English. There are many forms: *am, are, is, was, were, being,* and *been.* In this exercise you will be speaking in the first person, and you will use only *am* or *was.* The teacher will describe a situation. Pretend that you are very dissatisfied. You are also in a complaining mood, so think of all the things you can to complain about. Use such phrases as:

displeased with
dissatisfied with
bored with
tired of
surprised at
disappointed in
used to
interested in
accustomed to
disgusted with

In the examples, notice how *I'm* is used more frequently than the more formal *I am.*

Example:

Teacher: Your uncle gave you a necktie that you didn't like. You return it to the store.

Student A: My uncle gave me a necktie for my birthday. I am displeased with it. I'm going to return it to the store.

Student B: I was disappointed in the color of the necktie. It was so depressing. I get bored with dark colors.

Student C: I'm dissatisfied with its length. It is too short.

Student D: I'm disappointed in the material. It isn't heavy enough.

Student E: I'm surprised at the poor quality of the necktie. I am used to wearing nicer ones.

a. Your uncle bought you another present.
b. You attended a very bad lecture. The facts were incorrect and you didn't think that the lecturer's jokes were very funny.
c. You attended a poor movie.

d. You wanted to attend a particular college. You visited the college first and found that it was not what you had expected.
e. You have just eaten a meal that you didn't like. It cost you $11.00. The restaurant where you ate is a famous one.
f. You have just paid $3.00 to get your clothes from the cleaners. They are not at all clean.
g. You are driving your car down the street. You hear a big noise and suddenly your car stops. Just this morning you had it fixed at the best garage in town.

Exercise 2. Forms of *be + used to:*

The teacher will describe a situation. Answer the questions using some form of *be + used to.*

Examples:

Teacher: When you woke up this morning, the muscles in your shoulder were sore. It might have been because you were not used to something. Tell us some of the things which might have caused the soreness.

Student A: I'm not used to the damp weather here.

Student B: I went bowling yesterday and I'm not used to so much exercise.

Student C: I'm not used to sleeping near a window.

Student D: I'm not used to my new bed yet.

a. Susan came from a tropical country. Here it is very cold. Tell us some of the things that she isn't used to.
b. Jim went to the doctor because he didn't feel well. The doctor recommended a special diet. Tell us about some of the things Jim will have to get used to.
c. You've lost weight since being in the United States. It might be because of differences in food. Tell us about some of the foods you're not used to.
d. Nicole has been a teacher in France. Now she has come to the United States to be a student. Tell us about some of the things that she will have to become used to.
e. When Margaret was home she had three servants. But in the United States she must do her own work. Tell us about some of the things that Margaret isn't used to doing.
f. Robert has always worked quietly by himself. Now he has a job in a noisy factory where he must answer three telephones and must come when any of the workers call him. What will he have to get used to?

Exercise 3. Questions with *is* and *could it be:*

Think of a person who would be known by everyone in the class. Give a hint using *is*. When the other students try to guess who it is, they can ask questions using *is* or *could it be*. If you can't think of a person to talk about, you might choose one of these: Santa Claus, the President of the United States, the teacher, a person in your class, a famous movie star, or someone who is currently in the news.

Example:

Student A:	I am thinking of a person who is in this building.
Student B:	Is the person a man?
Student A:	Yes, he is a man.
Student C:	Is the person in this room?
Student A:	No, he is across the hall.
Student D:	Could it be the man who is in charge of the language laboratory?
Student A:	No, it is the man who helps the man who is in charge of the language laboratory.

Exercise 4. Forms of *be* and forms of *have* used with *still, already, anymore, yet:*

The teacher will make a statement which will tell you only the beginning of a situation. Figure out the rest of it by making up questions and answers. Since you will be talking about things dealing with time, you will probably find it helpful to use such words as *still, already, anymore,* and *yet.* If using all of these words is too confusing, begin by using only *already* and then come back and do the exercise again using the different terms.

Example:

Teacher:	The theater opens at 7:00. It is now 7:10.
Student A:	Are people going in already?
Student B:	Yes, some people are already in. Have you bought your ticket yet?
Student C:	Yes, I've bought mine already. Have you bought yours yet?
Student D:	No, I haven't bought it yet. Has the candy counter opened yet?
Student E:	Yes, it has already opened.

a. John wants to take his friend to a concert tonight.
b. Mary is planning to go to New York tomorrow.
c. You and your friends are supposed to meet at the park for a picnic at 5:00. It is now a quarter past five.
d. Richard is studying at the university. He is very good at mathematics but very slow at learning history.

e. Mary has been studying music since she was a child. Her sister began to study last month.
f. I just called a taxi. I hear an automobile horn.
g. I called a taxi an hour ago.
h. The lecturer has been talking for five hours.
i. The Lanes used to be very rich. They traveled a lot.
j. The swimming course was supposed to begin on Monday. Today is Wednesday. Bob wants to learn to swim and dive.

Exercise 5. More practice with *be* and *have* used in longer utterances with *still, already, anymore,* and *yet:*

This time the teacher will present two statements. Join them in a question using one of the words listed above. Ask another student. If he cannot give the appropriate answer, then he should say so and repeat the question to another student.

Example:

Teacher: Pierre Curie and Marie Sklodowska were married and worked in France. They are famous for their discovery of radium.

Student A: Were they already married when they discovered radium?

Student B: I'm not sure, but I don't think so. Were they already married?

or: I don't know if they had discovered radium yet.

or: Yes. I believe they were already married when they discovered it.

a. Louis Pasteur finished his studies at the Sorbonne. He became famous for his work with bacteria.
b. Marco Polo wrote about his adventures in China. Columbus wrote about his trip to the New World.
c. Abraham Lincoln became the 16th President of the United States. The Civil War began in 1860.
d. In the 1920's many miners suffered from silicosis. Preventive steps with aluminum dust were first taken in the late 1930's.
e. I wrote a letter to my parents. They sent me some money.
f. I applied for admission to one of the greatest universities in the United States. I passed my English course with honors.
g. I have a bad cold. I went swimming last Sunday.
h. I studied Spanish. My brother studied French.

Exercise 6. Forms of *be* in context:

In this essay there are many examples of various forms of the verb *be.* The essay has many details in it so that you might get good practice in taking notes while the teacher reads it to you. When he is finished, he will ask you to tell him about certain things.

THE PRESIDENTS OF THE UNITED STATES

The United States has had thirty-five Presidents. Grover Cleveland *was elected* as our 22nd and 24th President. The State Department has ruled that he *must be counted* twice. This means that the Office of President *has been filled* by thirty-five different men, but that Lyndon Johnson *is* our 36th President.

The first President, George Washington, *was inaugurated* in 1789. He served two terms that ended in 1797. When he died, he *was mourned* here and abroad as one of the great men of the time. He *was buried* at his home at Mount Vernon, Virginia, which *is* just outside Washington, D.C. Nine of our Presidents *have been elected* for two terms. Franklin D. Roosevelt served three full terms. He *was elected* to a fourth term in 1944. He died in 1945, and his term *was completed* by Harry Truman.

The shortest term *was served* by William Henry Harrison who died one month after his inauguration in 1841. Four Presidents *were assassinated* while in office. The first of these *was* our 16th President, Abraham Lincoln. He *was shot* while attending the theater in Washington. James Garfield *was shot* a few months after his inauguration and died at the age of forty-nine. William McKinley *was assassinated* in Buffalo, New York, in 1901. John Kennedy *was killed* in Texas in 1963.

James Buchanan *was* the only bachelor *to be elected.* He *was assisted* in the social activities of the White House by a niece who *is remembered* for her gracious manner as hostess.

One of our Presidents (Andrew Johnson) *had been employed* as a tailor before he became President. Three of our Presidents --Washington, Grant, and Eisenhower—*had been* Generals of the Army before they *were elected.*

Our 26th President, Theodore Roosevelt, *had been* a Colonel in the Army prior *to being elected* to serve as Vice-President during William McKinley's term of office. After President McKinley *was assassinated,* Theodore Roosevelt automatically became President. It *was* in this way that he became the youngest man ever *to be called upon* to fill the presidency. He *was* forty-two years old. John Kennedy *was* the youngest person *to be elected* to the office. He *was* forty-three at the time he *was chosen.*

The state of Virginia *is known* as the "Presidents' State." Eight of our Presidents *were born* in Virginia and seven *were born* in Ohio. Some of our Presidents *will be remembered* by future generations as great men of their times.

The teacher will repeat the phrase from the essay. Use it in a sentence. You needn't try to make your sentence exactly like the one in the original essay. Even if you are not consciously trying to use *be,* your sentence will probably contain a form of this very common verb.

Example:
Teacher: some of the Presidents
Student: Some of the Presidents will be remembered as great men.

a. Grover Cleveland counted twice
b. the 22nd and the 24th President
c. thirty-five different men
d. the first President
e. when he died
f. at his home at Mount Vernon
g. for two terms
h. three full terms
i. a fourth term in 1944
j. by Harry Truman
k. the shortest term
l. the assassination of
m. the only bachelor
n. the social activities of the White House
o. her gracious manner as hostess
p. a tailor
q. Generals of the Army
r. a Colonel
s. Vice-President with William McKinley
t. the youngest President
u. the youngest man to be elected
v. the "Presidents' State"
w. eight of the Presidents
x. seven of the Presidents

Now the teacher will repeat the clues. This time if you are called on, make up a question and ask another student. If he can't answer, then he should ask someone else.

Lesson Seventeen

REVIEW

Listen carefully as the teacher reads this essay about trips around the world. Afterwards you will be given a chance to talk about it using the patterns which you have practiced in earlier lessons.

TRIPS AROUND THE WORLD

In 1872, Jules Verne wrote a novel about a man whose name was Phineas Fogg. The remarkable Mr. Fogg made a trip around the world in order to win a bet. He traveled by boat, by horse-drawn coach, by elephant, and by any other means that he could find. He won the bet by making the trip in eighty days. All of that was just a story, but there are real facts about trips around the world which are equally interesting.

Magellan's ships were the first to circle the globe. They started out in 1519 and returned in 1522. Magellan was a Portuguese navigator in the service of Spain.

One of the earliest trips by a woman was undertaken by a newspaper reporter who wrote under the name of Nellie Bly. The courageous Nellie Bly made her trip in 1889. It required seventy-two days and six hours.

In 1926, a record was set by two men who made the trip in a little less than twenty-nine days. They went by train, by motor car, by plane, and by steamship.

The German dirigible, Graf Zeppelin, went around the world in 1929. This trip required twenty days. The dirigible stopped three times for fuel. In 1938, Howard Hughes made the trip by plane in a little less than four days. His plane stopped several times in order to refuel.

Before 1949, all planes that made the trip had to stop in order to refuel. The first non-stop trip was made in 1949. This flight was accomplished by refueling the plane in mid-air. Large flying tankers refueled the plane by connecting fuel lines to the flying plane.

The fastest trip by plane was made in 1957. Three U.S. Air Force jet planes flew around the world in forty-five hours, by refueling while they were in flight.

On April 12, 1961, Yuri Gagarin made a complete orbit of the earth by spacecraft. The complete flight lasted 108 minutes. It took eighty-nine minutes to make one orbit. This was certainly different from Nellie Bly's trip which required seventy-two days.

Exercise 1. Review of *that* + sentence:

The teacher will ask you what you know about something. Answer him with the *I know that + sentence* pattern.

Examples:

Teacher: What do you know about Jules Verne?
Student: I know that Jules Verne wrote a story about Phineas Fogg.

Teacher: What do you know about the remarkable Mr. Fogg?
Student: I know that the remarkable Mr. Fogg went around the world in eighty days.

Teacher: What do you know about how Mr. Fogg won a bet?
Student: I know that Phineas Fogg won a bet by making his trip around the world in eighty days.

a. What do you know about Mr. Fogg's trip?
b. What do you know about Magellan?
c. What do you know about a famous trip by a woman?
d. What do you know about Nellie Bly?
e. What do you know about the 1926 trip?
f. What do you know about the Graf Zeppelin?
g. What do you know about how many times the dirigible stopped for fuel?
h. What do you know about Howard Hughes' trip in 1938?
i. What do you know about what was necessary for all plane trips made before 1949?
j. What do you know about the first non-stop trip?
k. What do you know about the fastest trip by plane?
l. What do you know about what Yuri Gagarin did in 1961?
m. What do you know about Nellie Bly and Gagarin?

Exercise 2. Review of questions with *how, why, when, which, who,* and *what:*

Change the teacher's statement into a question beginning with *how, why, when, which, who,* or *what.* The student who answers should pick an appropriate pattern. Sometimes very short answers will be appropriate.

Example:

Teacher: Phineas Fogg traveled fast.
Student A: Why did Phineas Fogg travel fast?
Student B: So he could win a bet.
or
Student A: How did Phineas Fogg travel?

Student B: He traveled by boat, by horse-drawn coach, by elephant, and by any other method that he could find.

a. This trip took seventy-two days and six hours.
b. A trip around the world was made in 1926.
c. Another important trip was made in 1929.
d. Howard Hughes went around the world in 1938.
e. Hughes' plane stopped several times.
f. Before 1949 no plane could make a non-stop flight.
g. Today non-stop flights can be made.
h. The fastest trip by plane was made in 1957.
i. The Russian cosmonaut, Yuri Gagarin, made a complete orbit of the earth in eighty-nine minutes.

Exercise 3. Review of *before, after,* and *since:*

If there is room on the chalkboard, your teacher might put this chart up so that you can easily see it and talk about it. He will name one of the items as a reference point. Make up a sentence about something in the essay. Use *before, after,* or *since* depending on how your statement relates to the reference point named by the teacher.

1872	Jules Verne
1889	Nellie Bly
1926	29-day trip
1929	Graf Zeppelin
1938	Howard Hughes
1949	non-stop flight
1957	jet planes
1961	Yuri Gagarin

Example:

Teacher: the 1949 non-stop flight

Student A: Before the first non-stop flight made in 1949 it had been necessary for all planes to land for refueling.

Student B: Jet planes were able to make the trip much faster after people learned how to refuel in the air.

Student C: Since 1949 there have been many new developments.

Exercise 4. Review of *still, already, anymore,* and *yet:*

Referring to this same chart, make up a question using *still, already, anymore,* or *yet.* These words can also be used in answering the questions.

Examples:

Student A: Had Jules Verne still not written his book by 1873?
Student B: No, it was already written by 1873.

Student C: Was it still necessary to land for fuel in 1953?
Student D: No, it wasn't necessary anymore.

Student E: In 1926 was it still necessary to plan on a month for the trip?
Student F: No, this wasn't necessary anymore.

Student G: Was it possible to make non-stop trips in 1930?
Student H: No, it wasn't possible yet.

You might also ask each other questions about events in your lives or in your home countries as they relate to the events on the chart.

Examples:

Student A: Were people already making non-stop trips when you were born?
Student B: No, this hadn't happened yet.

Student C: When you came to the United States were jet planes being used?
Student D: Yes, jet planes were already being used, but we didn't refuel in air.

Exercise 5. Review of *too, either,* and *but:*

The teacher will name two different people or activities which were mentioned in the essay. Make up a sentence using *either, too,* or *but.*

Examples:

Teacher: Phineas Fogg and Nellie Bly
Student: Phineas Fogg was a fictional character but Nellie Bly wasn't.

Teacher: Howard Hughes and Nellie Bly
Student: Howard Hughes went around the world and Nellie Bly did too.

Teacher: Travel by elephant and travel by spacecraft
Student: Travel by elephant isn't very comfortable and travel by spacecraft isn't either.

a. Hughes' plane and the dirigible
b. Hughes' plane and the jet planes
c. Nellie Bly and the jet planes

d. the jet planes and Phineas Fogg
e. Yuri Gagarin and Howard Hughes
f. Yuri Gagarin and Nellie Bly
g. travel by elephant and travel by motor car
h. travel by steamship and travel by spacecraft
i. an astronaut and Magellan

Lesson Eighteen

THE VERB *Wish*

Exercise 1. *I wish* + statement:

Although the verb *wish* is sometimes used to mean *want*, e.g. *I wish to go home*, the most common usage is in a sentence pattern such as *I wish that* + statement. This is the same pattern which you have studied earlier with other verbs. You probably remember that in this pattern the *that* can be deleted. You will delete it in this lesson because you will soon be practicing patterns which are similar, but which cannot take *that*. It will be easier if you become accustomed to the pattern without *that*.

Pretend that you have three wishes for yourself, your family, or your country and its people. When the teacher calls on you, tell him what you wish. Try to make your wishes different from those of your classmates'. Use the *I wish* + statement pattern.

Examples:

Student A: I wish I had a million dollars.
I wish I was beautiful.
I wish I had a Cadillac with gold wheels.

Student B: I wish all my countrymen were rich.
I wish the country people didn't have to work so hard.
I wish we had snow in my country.

Exercise 2. Questions with *wish:*

Everyone in the class should think of a favorite daydream. Try to guess what each person's daydream is. In asking the questions, use a pattern of *do you wish* + statement.

Example:

Student A: I have a favorite daydream. Guess what it is.
Student B: Do you wish you were handsome?
Student A: Sometimes, but that's not it.
Student C: Do you wish you were younger?
Student A: No, I like my age.
Student D: Do you wish you were married?
Student A: Never!
Student E: Do you wish you were a millionaire?
Student A: That's it, I wish I was very rich.

Exercise 3. *Wish* + statement with past time expression:

The teacher will make a comment about something that has already happened. Make up a question using *wish.* When a student answers your question, he should also use *wish.* Because this is conversation practice, you will probably want to use contractions such as *He'd* and *She'd* rather than *He had* and *She had.* Several of you can make up questions about the same situation.

Example:

Teacher:	Jim missed a good party last night.
Student A:	Does he wish he'd gone?
Student B:	Yes, he does. He wishes he'd gone.
Student C:	Does he wish he'd been invited?
Student D:	Of course he does. He wishes he'd been invited.
Student E:	Does he wish he could have gone?
Student F:	Yes, he does. He wishes he could have gone.

a. Bill lost his wallet at the football game last week.
b. Mrs. Lane dented the fender of her husband's car yesterday.
c. Jimmy disobeyed his mother and got his new suit dirty. She spanked him.
d. Several small boys were chasing a dog when it bit the youngest boy.
e. We went to a very expensive restaurant last night. The food was terrible.
f. You ran into an old friend who wanted to borrow a hundred dollars from you.
g. You bought a new car without shopping around. The car is not satisfactory.

Exercise 4. *Wish* in conversation:

To get you started thinking the teacher will name some famous people. Tell what they probably wished.

Example:

Teacher:	Madame Curie
Student:	Madame Curie probably wished that her husband had lived longer.

a. the captain of the Titanic
b. Handel's father
c. Napoleon
d. Marc Antony
e. Mary Todd Lincoln

Continue by talking about people who are in the news now, or famous people from your own country. Where necessary, give a brief explanation so that your classmates will know why the person wished what he did.

Lesson Nineteen

THE PATTERN OF *See Someone Go*, CONTRASTED WITH *Urge Someone To Go*

Exercise 1. Verb + Noun Phrase + Verb:

The teacher will name two verbs. Make up a sentence using the two verbs. Put a noun phrase between them. Feel free to change the tense or the number of the verb.

Examples:
Teacher: make—go
Student: I can't make my car go.

Teacher: watch—fly
Student: Have you ever watched a model airplane fly?

a. make—run
b. let—see
c. hear—growl
d. help—find
e. see—crash
f. let—move
g. hear—speak
h. watch—win
i. make—practice

Exercise 2. Verb + noun phrase + *to* + verb:

There are many verbs which act much like the ones in the above exercise, except that they require a *to* in front of the second verb. This time when the teacher names two verbs, make up a sentence using the pattern of verb + noun phrase + *to* + verb.

Examples:
Teacher: want—come
Student: I want Sally to come with us.

Teacher: persuade—give
Student: Please persuade the teacher to give us all A's.

a. urge—come
b. get—vote
c. advise—pick up
d. order—get out
e. expect—win
f. want—dance
g. permit—leave

h. ask--babysit
i. invite—eat
j. pay—translate
k. permit—join
l. tell—dig
m. encourage—learn
n. order—report
o. advise--withdraw
p. hire—paint

Exercise 3. Verb + noun phrase + *to* + verb contrasted with verb + noun phrase + verb:

This time the teacher will make up a sentence. Then he will name another verb. Change his sentence to include the new verb in place of the first verb in the set. Your meaning will not be the same. Also, feel free to change the tense of the verbs. You will have to be careful in deciding whether or not to use *to*. If you have trouble look at the list given in Exercise 4.

Example:

Teacher: I want John to run.
Student A: I saw John run.

Teacher: ask
Student B: I asked John to run.

Teacher: order
Student C: I ordered John to run.

Teacher: make
Student D: I made John run.

a. He made the boys walk every day.
got
permit
let
tell
help

b. The librarian ordered Sam to turn in his books.
ask
make
let
want

c. Did you hear Professor Stone speak?
expect
tell
see
choose

d. My landlady invited me to eat dinner last night.
order
let
watch
ask

e. Jim said he saw the airplane crash into the building.
want
hear
make
watch

f. The man I live with heard a tiger growl in the night.
make
get
want
see

g. My favorite teacher asked me to drive her home.
order
let
permit
made
choose

h. That woman expects her daughter to win the beauty contest.
watch
see
want
tell
permit

i. My roommate will encourage me to write my paper.
teach
watch
make
help

Exercise 4. These patterns in conversation:

The teacher will describe a situation. Use your imagination and make up sentences about it. Try to use some of the verbs and the patterns which we have been practicing. Perhaps the teacher will put these lists on the board to help you.

Verbs used with *to*

advise	*invite*
ask	*order*
choose	*permit*
encourage	*persuade*
expect	*teach*
get	*tell*
help	*urge*
hire	*want*

Verbs used alone

have
hear
help
let
make
see

Example:

Teacher: A mother wants her young son to go to school, but he doesn't want to.
Student A: She expects her son to go to school, but he doesn't want to.
Student B: She asks him to go. She begs him to go, but he doesn't want to go.
Student C: She urges him to go.
Student D: He wishes he didn't have to go.
Student E: His mother expects him not to go.
Student F: She tries to make him go, but he refuses.
Student G: She spanks him and makes him go.

a. A farmer is trying to get his donkey into the barn. The animal is very stubborn.
b. A father knows all boys need a college education but he doesn't have enough money to send his son to college.
c. A little boy is lost. Fortunately, he sees a policeman who can help him.
d. A mother has not received a letter from her son for several months. She knows her son is very lazy.
e. Mary had a birthday last week. She needed a new typewriter. She had told her father that she needed one but she didn't get it for her birthday.
f. John took Mary to a night club where a famous orchestra was playing. Mary likes to dance and is especially fond of waltzes.

Lesson Twenty

MODALS WITH PAST TENSE

Exercise 1. Use of *should* with past tense:

Many times after something has happened, people make all kinds of suggestions about what should have been done. We call these belated suggestions because they come too late to help the situation. In this exercise the teacher will briefly describe a situation. Use your imagination and see what belated suggestions you can make. Use *should* or *shouldn't* in your suggestions.

Example:

Teacher:	John failed a history examination today. He was visiting friends in Detroit yesterday.
Student A:	He should have studied, but he didn't.
Student B:	He shouldn't have gone to Detroit.
Student C:	He shouldn't have been visiting friends, but he was.
Student D:	He should have memorized his notes, but he didn't.
Student E:	He shouldn't have wasted his time visiting.
Student F:	He didn't pass the examination, but he should have.

a. Last winter Bob was skating when the ice broke under him. There was a sign which warned, "Thin Ice".
b. Jim got into trouble last week when he used the rent money to bet on a horse race. His horse came in last.
c. Margaret put her purse down in a store while she tried on dresses. Now she can't find it.
d. Richard doesn't have a driver's license, but he took a friend's car to Detroit. He was arrested.
e. John washed his new red shirt with all of the other clothes. Now everything is pink.
f. Mr. Brown invested a lot of money in certain stocks that newspapers showed were losing value.
g. George Frederick Handel's father wouldn't permit him to study music.
h. Several hundred children drowned last year. The reason was either that their parents were not careful or that they had not been taught to swim.
i. People in California build their homes on steep mountain slopes. Some of the homes collapse during heavy rains.
j. One of the southern states built a beautiful turnpike. All of its overpasses were two feet lower than the maximum

height allowed for trucks. Regulations for trucks were listed in the state traffic code.

Exercise 2. Questions and answers with *should have:*

This time when the teacher describes a situation, make up a question using *should have* or *shouldn't have.* The student who answers should also try to use these words. Several questions can be asked about each situation.

Example:

Teacher: Jimmy hadn't learned how to swim. He disobeyed his mother one day and went down by the river to play. He fell in. There were some men working nearby who rescued him.
Student A: Should he have obeyed his mother?
Student B: Yes, he should have.
Student C: Should he have disobeyed his mother?
Student D: No, he shouldn't have.
Student E: Should he have been playing by the river?
Student F: No, he shouldn't have.
Student G: Should he have been playing at home?
Student H: Yes, he should have.
Student I: Should he have shouted for help?
Student J: Yes, he should have.
Student K: Should the men have rescued him?
Student L: Yes, they should have.

a. Margaret, who was wearing a dark hat and coat, crossed a rainy street one night. She had seen that the light was red but she walked across anyway. A man who was driving sixty miles an hour almost hit her.
b. Mary had a bad cold last week. Her doctor had told her to stay in bed until she was well, but she got up and went to a dance. She has pneumonia now.
c. John told his father last summer that he wanted to go to college this year. His father replied that in order to do this John must work and save his money. The boy didn't listen.
d. Jimmy didn't obey his mother. He took a short cut from school and got lost on his way home last Friday.
e. Mrs. Smith didn't like banks. She kept her money and other valuables in a box under her bed. One night the house burned while she was out.

Exercise 3. Questions and answers with *could have:*

This time the teacher will describe a situation where someone has a problem which needs solving. Ask questions which might lead to a satisfactory solution. Use *could have* in your questions. Also be thinking of situations which you might describe after the teacher has finished with his examples.

Example:

Teacher:	A traveler came to a deep swift river. There were large rocks in the river and tall trees along the banks. The traveler had an ax, a rope, and two sticks. How could he have gotten across?
Student A:	Could he have swum across?
Teacher:	No, he couldn't have. The river was too swift.
Student B:	Could he have waded across?
Teacher:	No, he couldn't have. The water was too deep.
Student C:	Could he have jumped from rock to rock?
Teacher:	No, he couldn't have. They were too far apart.
Student D:	Could he have built a boat?
Teacher:	Yes, he could have, but he didn't.
Student E:	Could he have built a bridge?
Teacher:	Not exactly. This is really an old riddle or joke. The answer is that he could have gotten a cross by making one out of two sticks.

a. John and Mary quarreled. He had a lot of trouble making up with her but they are friends now. What could he have done?
b. It was 8:00 and Margaret had to be in Detroit by 9:30. How could she have gotten there?
c. A man was in prison. The walls were thick and the windows had bars across them. The prison was surrounded by a high wall and was in the middle of a lake. How could the prisoner have escaped?
d. Two boys were lost in a cave. They had a flashlight, several long pieces of string, and some newspapers. How could they have found their way out of the cave?

Students continue by posing their problems and giving the appropriate answers.

Exercise 4. Use of *might have:*

There are times in all of our lives when we are faced with several possibilities. Many of the famous men and women of history missed opportunities for one reason or another. What possibilities can you think of in connection with the following people? Use *might have* in your sentences.

Example:

Teacher:	Napoleon Bonaparte who wanted to conquer the world

Student A: Napoleon might have conquered all of Europe, but he was defeated at Waterloo.
Student B: He might have been Emperor of Europe, but the British forces defeated him.
Student C: He might have been killed in battle, but he wasn't.
Student D: He might not have died a prisoner, if he hadn't been defeated.

a. Pierre Curie, the great French physicist, who was accidentally killed when he was forty-seven
b. the German musician, Robert Schumann, who permanently damaged one of his fingers while he was practicing the piano
c. the Titanic, which sank after it had struck an iceberg
d. T. S. Eliot, an American who lives and writes in England
e. doctors who had to experiment for many years before they found a polio vaccine
f. Balboa, who was not able to establish a successful colony because fire destroyed it
g. President Kennedy, who was assassinated during his first term in office
h. Abraham Lincoln, who was assassinated before the Civil War Reconstruction
i. Joan of Arc, who was executed after she had helped her country
j. Thomas Edison, who was fired from his first job
k. Handel's father, who didn't like him to practice

Exercise 5. Use of *must have:*

The teacher will briefly describe two incidents. Be a detective and figure out what must have happened. As he gives you more clues, continue figuring out the details. Use *must have* in your statements:

Example:

Teacher: You come home and find that everything is all upset. All of the drawers and cabinets are open and the contents are scattered about the house.
Student: Someone must have been in my house.
Teacher: There are muddy footprints near a window.
Student: He must have come in through a window.

a. There is an empty Coke bottle in the kitchen.
b. The kitchen stove is still warm.
c. There is part of a sandwich on the table.
d. Your child's bank has been opened.
e. One of your suits is missing.

f. An expensive vase has been dropped and broken.
g. A cigarette is still burning in an ashtray.
h. The cigarette has lipstick on it.
i. The back door of your house is open.

You decide to buy a second-hand car. It originally cost $5000. The dealer tells you that he got the car from the original owner.

a. The car is in very poor condition.
b. The tires are badly worn.
c. The front bumper is bent.
d. One of the windows won't open.
e. Several small holes have been burned in the front seat.
f. You find a doll and a ball behind the back seat.
g. You find several maps of California in the glove compartment.
h. The front seat has been moved forward as far as it will go.

Exercise 6. Modals with past tense in conversation:

Since the purpose of this class is to prepare you to converse freely in English, it is helpful to practice spontaneous conversation as well as the controlled conversation which you have had in most of the other lessons. Printed here is a conversation which was held in one class which was practicing modals. Perhaps your class can have a similar conversation. You might talk about a party or about some other recent event which people in your class went to. Of course your conversation won't be exactly like this one. This is just an example so that you and your teacher can see how this type of thing might be worked out. The faster you can answer the questions and the faster the teacher can ask them, the more natural the conversation will be.

Teacher: Foreign students studying in the U.S.A. have many opportunities to practice English in social situations. They frequently receive invitations to dinner or to parties. All of you received an invitation to attend a party at the Union the other night.

Teacher: Should foreign students attend social events?
Student: Yes, they should.
Teacher: Should they be afraid to go?
Student: No, they shouldn't.
Teacher: Should the students go when they are invited to a party?
Student: Yes, of course. They should go to the party.
Teacher: Why?
Student: To practice their English. To have a good time.

Teacher: The party at the Union was very interesting. All of the students were invited. I don't believe that anyone was ill. None of the students had other appointments. But Christina and Maria were not at the party. A friend told me that they were visiting friends from their own country. What should they have been doing?
Student: They should have been attending the party.
Teacher: Should they have been visiting friends?
Student: No, they shouldn't have.
Teacher: Were they invited?
Student: Yes, they were.
Teacher: Were they ill?
Student: No, they weren't.
Teacher: Could they have gone?
Student: Yes, they could have.
Teacher: Should they have gone?
Student: Yes, they should have.
Teacher: Did they go?
Student: No, they didn't.
Teacher: There were many people at the party. I didn't see all of them. For example, I didn't see Halim. He might have been there, but I didn't see him. Did you see Halim?
Student: He might have been there, but I didn't see him.
Teacher: Was Carmen dancing?
Student: She might have been dancing, but I didn't see her.
Teacher: Did Mr. Wall speak on the program?
Student: He might have spoken, but I didn't hear him.
Teacher: Did Mr. Johnson bring a girlfriend?
Student: He might have brought one, but I didn't see her.
Teacher: Did they play a lot of fast dances?
Student: They might have played a lot, but I didn't hear them.
Teacher: Was everybody practicing English?
Student: They might have been practicing, but I didn't hear them.
Teacher: I saw Jose and Julio in a corner. Should they have been speaking Spanish?
Student: No, they shouldn't have been speaking Spanish. They should have been practicing English.
Teacher: Were they speaking Spanish?
Student: Yes, they were.
Teacher: Should they have been practicing English?
Student: Yes, they should have.
Teacher: Were they practicing English?

Student: No, they weren't.
Teacher: There were many English speakers at the party.
Student: Rachel and Vera could have been practicing English, but they weren't.
Teacher: Could they have been practicing?
Student: Yes, they could have.
Teacher: Were they practicing English?
Student: No, they weren't.
Teacher: I didn't see Mr. Sato at the party. I saw his coat and I thought I heard his voice. He must have been there, but I didn't see him. I saw Yoko several times before ten o'clock. I didn't see her after ten.
Student: She must have gone home at ten.
Teacher: All of the coffee was gone when I went to the refreshment table. Which beverage do you think the guests preferred?
Student: They must have liked the coffee.
Teacher: There was plenty of tea left. Do you still think that everyone must have preferred coffee?
Student: Yes, they must have.
Teacher: The dancing continued until 1:30. Do you think they liked it?
Student: Yes, they must have enjoyed it.
Teacher: Mohamed ate four pieces of cake. Do you think he liked it?
Student: Yes, he must have liked the cake.
Teacher: Ivan was sad all through the party. Why do you think he was sad?
Student: He must have been thinking about his girlfriend.
Teacher: Takuji talked all evening with a beautiful American girl. Do you think he learned a lot of English?
Student: Yes, he must have learned a lot of English. He must have liked her, too.
Teacher: Grethe went home early. Do you suppose she was tired?
Student: Yes, she must have been tired.

Lesson Twenty-one

SUBORDINATING CONJUNCTIONS

Exercise 1. Use of *whenever, unless, although,* and *because:*

The teacher will make two statements. Make them into one sentence by adding *whenever, unless, although,* or *because.* Usually you can attach the word to the beginning of the sentence, but sometimes it can go between the two clauses.

a. Napoleon was defeated. He was very powerful.
b. Julius Caesar was assassinated by his fellow statesmen. He had trusted them.
c. Robert Schumann became a famous musician. He injured his finger and could not play the piano.
d. More than 1500 people lost their lives. The Titanic didn't have enough lifeboats.
e. He usually had a cigar in his mouth. Sometimes we saw him without it when he was eating a meal.
f. Prime Minister Nehru sometimes became angry with newspapermen. He was usually a friendly man.
g. We don't always receive letters. The mailman comes every day.
h. People get seriously ill. They see a doctor.
i. We won't get a traffic ticket. We have broken the law.
j. People disobey the traffic laws. They can get a ticket.
k. We shouldn't get a ticket. We have failed to obey the laws.
l. Children continue to get polio. Salk vaccine is generally available.
m. Hawaii is our youngest state. It achieved statehood last.

Exercise 2. Use of *although, because, whether or not, if,* and *whenever:*

The teacher will say the first clause of a sentence. Finish it for him by adding *although* and making up an appropriate clause. Do the same for each of the five words you are practicing. Perhaps the teacher will list the words on the board.

Example:

Teacher: They walk every day

Student: They walk every day, although they are very busy.

They walk every day, because they need the exercise.

Student: They walk every day, whether or not the weather is good.
They walk every day, if the weather is good.
They walk every day, whenever they find time.

a. People must pay income tax . . .
b. Children should obey their parents . . .
c. If you buy a new car, you should inspect it carefully . . .
d. Jan usually prepares very bad dinners for her husband . . .
e. Poor drivers should have their licenses taken away . . .
f. George Frederick Handel practiced in the attic at night . . .
g. Some people buy expensive automobiles . . .
h. Winston Churchill usually had a cigar in his mouth . . .
i. Little boys like ice cream . . .

Exercise 3. Use of *because of* and *because of the fact that:*

The teacher will make a statement. Make up a related fact and join it to his sentence with *because.* A second student should repeat your sentence only putting *because* at the beginning, instead of the middle of the sentence. A third student rewords the sentence using *because of* in the middle of the sentence. And then a fourth student rewords it using *because of* at the beginning of the sentence. Perhaps this chart will help you.

Student A: Statement + *because* + Statement
Student B: *Because* + Statement + Statement
Student C: Statement + *because of* + Noun Phrase
Student D: *Because of* + Noun Phrase + Statement

If you find it hard to change a statement into a Noun Phrase to go with *because of,* then you can use *because of the fact that.*

Example:
Teacher: Deserts are very dry.
Student A: Deserts are very dry because they don't get much rain.
Student B: Because they don't get much rain, deserts are very dry.
Student C: Deserts are very dry because of the lack of rain.
or: Deserts are very dry because of the fact that they don't get much rain.
Student D: Because of the lack of rain, deserts are very dry.
or: Because of the fact that they don't get much rain, deserts are very dry.

a. The people of Texas used to be very proud.
b. Columbus wanted to make his voyage.

c. A city needs a police force.
d. People should learn foreign languages.
e. Young people should try to go to college.
f. Parents take care of their children.
g. People should save money.
h. Space scientists will continue to launch rockets.
i. People shake hands.
j. It is difficult to become a doctor.
k. Children need to drink milk.
l. People learn a lot from television.

Exercise 4. Use of *although* and *in spite of:*

This exercise is similar to the preceding one, only this time use *although* to join the two statements. The second student uses *although* at the beginning of the sentence. The third student uses *in spite of* to join the two parts and the fourth student uses *in spite of* at the beginning of the sentence. Here is a chart which you might want to refer to.

Student A; Statement + *although* + Statement
Student B: *Although* + Statement + Statement
Student C: Statement + *in spite of* + Noun Phrase
Student D: *In spite of* + Noun Phrase + Statement

Here if you find it hard to change a statement into a Noun Phrase to go with *in spite of,* you can use *in spite of the fact that.*

Example:
Teacher: Many children refuse to eat spinach.
Student A: Many children refuse to eat spinach although it is good for them.
Student B: Although spinach is good for them many children refuse to eat it.
Student C: Many children refuse to eat spinach in spite of its food value.
or: Many children refuse to eat spinach in spite of the fact that it is good for them.
Student D: In spite of its food value many children refuse to eat spinach.
or: In spite of the fact that spinach is good for them many children refuse to eat it.

a. Many fat people eat lots of sweet things.
b. President Roosevelt was elected for four terms.
c. George Frederick Handel practiced in the attic of his home.
d. Some children don't want to go to school.
e. Many young brides don't cook very well.

f. Young people sometimes marry too early.
g. Some people don't pay their income tax.
h. Many crops were bad this year.
i. There are far too many traffic accidents.
j. People sometimes keep large sums of money in their homes.
k. Many people throughout the world are starving.

Exercise 5. Subordinating conjunctions in context:

Listen as your teacher reads this story. When he finishes, you can talk about it. As he reads it, listen for the conjunctions which you have been studying.

MR. SMITH BLUNDERS

Mr. Smith is well known in Washington *because* of his many social blunders. He always likes to attend the various social functions *because* he wants to expand his circle of friends. *Whenever* he is invited, he goes, *unless* he is ill.

Recently he received an invitation to a fashionable banquet. *Although* he did not know the hostess, he accepted the invitation. He was secretly very pleased, *because* he felt that his reputation as a desirable guest was growing.

When he arrived at the banquet hall, he found that about one hundred people had been invited. He began to move around the hall. He spoke to other guests *whether* he knew them *or not.* He soon realized that he had never met any of the other people present, *although* they seemed to know each other.

At dinner, he was seated beside a very dignified woman. The woman tried to be friendly *even though* she had never met Mr. Smith before. She spoke politely, *whenever* he spoke to her. Between the first and second course of the meal, she turned to Mr. Smith and said, "Do you see that gray-haired man at the end of the table? The one with the glasses."

"Ah, yes. Who is he?" asked Smith.

"He's the Secretary of the Interior!" she replied.

Mr. Smith said: "So that's the Secretary of the Interior! I'm afraid that I find very little to admire about him, *although* he is the Secretary."

The woman stiffened and did not reply. Smith continued *in spite of* her coldness. "I really can't see how he received his appointment, *unless* he is perhaps a relative of the President."

"It hardly matters *whether* you like the Secretary *or not,*" she said. "He was chosen *because* the President thought he was the man for the job. *If* he does the job well, you should have no complaint."

"That's just it," persisted Smith. "No one does the things he does, *unless* he is a complete fool!"

"Sir!" said the woman in all her dignity. "Do you know who I am?"

"No," replied Smith.

"I am the Secretary's wife," she said coldly. Mr. Smith was flabbergasted, but he went on *in spite of* his embarrassment.

"Madam, do you know who I am?"

"No, I don't," the woman replied.

"Thank goodness!" exclaimed Mr. Smith, as he quickly left the table.

In answering the teacher's questions, try to use one of the words you have been practicing. Afterwards, it might be fun for two of you to act out the conversation between the Secretary's wife and Mr. Smith.

a. What can you tell about Mr. Smith's reputation for making social blunders?
b. What does he like to do to expand his circle of friends?
c. When does he refuse invitations?
d. Why did Mr. Smith accept the invitation to this banquet?
e. Why was he secretly pleased?
f. Were there about a hundred people invited that evening?
g. Did he stand in a corner and not speak to the other guests?
h. Had he ever met any of the other guests?
i. Was it a very dignified woman who sat beside him or a sweet young girl?
j. How did she act toward Mr. Smith when they first sat down? Was she friendly? Did she speak politely?
k. What happened between the first and second courses?
l. Who did Mr. Smith think was a complete fool?
m. Why was Mr. Smith flabbergasted?

Lesson Twenty-two

SEQUENCES OF TENSES USED WITH *If*

Exercise 1. *If* used with future tense verbs:

When the teacher asks a question, answer it by making a brief statement about someone. Another student should repeat your statement adding an *if*-clause. Several of you might add different *if*-clauses, or you could make up a new answer to the teacher's question.

Example:

Teacher: What will John do tomorrow?
Student A: He'll get up at 8:00 . . .
Student B: He'll get up at 8:00 if he feels well.
Student C: He'll get up at 8:00 if he hears the alarm.
Student D: He'll get up at 8:00 if he doesn't oversleep.
Student E: He'll get up at 8:00 if he has a class.

Student F: John will register tomorrow . . .
Students continue.

a. What will you do after class?
b. What is the new police commissioner going to do?
c. What will the social committee do?
d. What is your uncle planning to do?
e. I saw workmen in your room last night. I wonder what they are going to do.
f. What is your landlady planning to do?

Exercise 2. *If* used in conditional statements:

Answer the teacher's question in a complete statement. Use *if* in your sentence.

Example:

Teacher: Where would you be now if you were President of the United States?
Student: If I were President of the United States, I would be in Washington, D. C.
or: I would be in the White House if I were President of the United States.

a. Where would you be now if you were . . .
   a policeman?
   a movie actor?
   a radio commentator?

b. What would John do tomorrow if he were . . .
   a detective?
   a mechanic?
   a teacher at the English Language Institute?
   an orchestra conductor?
   a soldier?
   a carpenter?

c. What would you do next week if you met . . .
   a beautiful movie star?
   the President of the U. S.?
   a man from Mars?
   an old friend from your country?
   a lion?
   an escaped convict?

d. What could you use if you wanted to . . .
   open a bottle?
   drive a nail into a piece of wood?
   draw a circle?
   remove a screw?
   write a letter?
   open a locked door?

Exercise 3. If in conversation:

The teacher will name two things, which will probably suggest an idea to you. Make up a sentence about them using *if*.

Examples:

Teacher: a Cadillac and $10,000
Student: If I had $10,000, I could easily buy a Cadillac.

Teacher: home and a plane ticket
Student: I couldn't go home if I got to the airport without my ticket.

a. your girlfriend and the movies
b. being happy and English
c. sick and sad
d. a rain coat and rain
e. cold and an overcoat
f. a swim and the beach
g. a crown and a king
h. a horse and a ride
i. an actor and handsome
j. a concert and two tickets
k. space flight and astronauts
l. a musician and practice
m. livestock and a farm
n. a doctor and disease
o. a delegate to the United Nations and peace

Exercise 4. *If* used with past time expressions:

It is sometimes said that *if* is the biggest word in the language. This only means that many things might happen or might have happened if circumstances were, or had been different, at a particular time. What *if*-statements can you make about the following people and events? Several of you can make up sentences about the same thing. Try to use *would have, might have,* or *could have* in your statements.

Example:

Teacher: Julius Caesar

Student A: If he hadn't been assassinated, Julius Caesar might have been the most important man in history.

Student B: Julius Caesar wouldn't have been killed if some people hadn't been jealous.

Students continue.

a. Julius Caesar
b. the earthquake that ruined San Francisco
c. the woman who didn't believe in banks
d. the man who bet the rent money
e. Christopher Columbus
f. Napoleon Bonaparte
g. the flowers that you forgot to put in water
h. the children who didn't learn to swim
i. the farmer who forgot to lock the barn door

Exercise 5. *If* in context:

Listen to this story as the teacher reads it out loud. When he is finished, you can talk about it. Notice the use of *if* as well as the different forms of modals which you have been practicing.

HERO OF THE SOUTH POLE

The English explorer, Captain Robert F. Scott, wanted to be the first man to reach the South Pole. The year 1910 brought Scott the chance for his great adventure. He was chosen to be leader of an Antarctic exploring party. *If* he had known what the adventure was to cost him, it is probable that he would never have accepted the opportunity.

Scott planned to take only a few dogs on the expedition, although most Arctic explorers had depended on dogs. Scott decided to use ponies for pulling the equipment. Several friends advised him to forget about the ponies. He should have listened to his friends, but he didn't. *If* he had listened to their advice he would have saved himself both time and trouble.

While Scott's ship was being loaded in New Zealand, some bad news came. Ronald Amundsen cabled that he was setting out from Norway to discover the South Pole. Scott went ahead with his plans in spite of this unwelcome news. He was certain that he would arrive at the Pole first, even *if* Amundsen had gotten a head-start.

The Terra Nova sailed on November 29, 1910. It arrived at the mountainous coast of the Antarctic on New Year's Day, 1911. The place where the boat stopped was 800 miles from the South Pole, but that was as far as they could go by water.

The men were able to build several camps along the route to the Pole before the long winter began. *If* there had been more time, they would have built more camps. They should have built more, because they needed them.

The winter lasted from April to August—four months of complete darkness. The men kept busy in spite of the long months of darkness. Even though the party did not set out for the Pole until November, there was still much work to be done.

Scott was sure of success because of his idea about the ponies. After only a few days of travel, he began to realize that the ponies had been a mistake. These little animals, with their long slender legs, could not walk very well in the snow. Many of the ponies got sick. *If* they had been accustomed to the cold weather, they wouldn't have gotten sick. Finally, it was necessary to kill the ponies. Scott had brought only a few dogs. *If* he had brought more dogs, they could have pulled the equipment. Because there were not enough dogs, the men had to pull the equipment.

Every few days, Scott sent a group of men back to the home camp. Finally, there were only five men left to make the last dash to the Pole. On January 15, 1912, the five men saw something black ahead of them. As they hurried toward the black speck, they saw that it was a black flag. The flag wouldn't have been there *if* Amundsen had not arrived ahead of them.

A few miles farther on, they found the Norwegian flag raised over a tent, because Amundsen had arrived first. He had left them a note. *If* they had arrived only sixteen hours earlier, they would have been the first men at the South Pole. *If* Scott had not insisted on the ponies, the British explorers would have arrived first.

Perhaps you know the rest of the story already. The trip back was disastrous. Two of the five men died from exposure after only a few days on the return journey. The fuel oil which had been stored at each of the camps had evaporated. There was hardly enough in the fuel tanks to warm a cup of water for the men. *If* there had not been so many blizzards, the three men might have been able to get back safely. As it was, Scott and his two companions died less than a hundred miles from the home camp. Although search parties went out to look for them, it was too late. Captain Scott's diary, found beside his body, told the whole story.

When the teacher mentions a phrase from the story, tell him something about it. You needn't use his exact words. Only sometimes will it be possible to use *if* in your sentence.

Example:

Teacher: wanted to be the first man

Student: Captain Scott wanted to be the first man to find the South Pole, but so did Ronald Amundsen.

a. the year that brought Scott the chance for his great adventure.
b. what the adventure was to cost him
c. most Arctic explorers
d. the advice of Scott's friends
e. Scott's ship being loaded
f. Ronald Amundsen's cable
g. unwelcome news that arrived
h. Scott being certain
i. the mountainous coast
j. what happened 800 miles from the Pole
k. more time and more camps
l. several camps along the route
m. their need for more camps
n. the winter
o. the fact that there was still much work to be done
p. their chance of success
q. a mistake
r. slender legs
s. being accustomed to cold weather
t. the need for more dogs
u. not enough dogs
v. sending groups of men
w. when there were only five men left
x. the black speck
y. how the flag got there
z. the Norwegian flag
aa. a note
bb. how much earlier they should have arrived
cc. the consequences of insisting on the ponies
dd. the disastrous trip back
ee. two of the five men
ff. fuel oil
gg. blizzards

hh. less than a hundred miles from home camp
ii. search parties
jj. Captain Scott's diary

Now when the teacher mentions something from the essay, use the phrase to ask another student a question.

Example:
Teacher: depended on dogs
Student A: Did Scott depend on dogs?
Student B: No, he thought he had a better idea. He took ponies.

a. in order to be the first
b. in the year 1910
c. if Scott had realized all of the possibilities
d. most Arctic explorers
e. his friends and their good advice
f. while the ship was being loaded
g. Ronald Amundsen's cable
h. Scott's idea for transportation
i. home camp 800 miles from the Pole
j. more camps on the route
k. they didn't build enough camps
l. four months of winter
m. the men were not bored
n. the greatest mistake
o. because of slender legs
p. because they weren't accustomed to the cold
q. more dogs needed
r. the black speck
s. Amundsen's note
t. disaster
u. two developments that Scott couldn't foresee
v. two of the five men
w. less than a hundred miles from home camp
x. the search parties' arrival
y. the diary

This time when the teacher calls on you, see if you can make some statements about this unfortunate experience without any prompting.

Lesson Twenty-three

COMPARISONS WITH *So* AND *Such*

Exercise 1. *So* + Adj + *that* + statement and *such* + noun phrase + *that* + statement:

In very casual American English, speakers will often make such statements as, "I want to thank you so much for the lovely gift," or "He is such a nice person" (usually said with emphasis on *such*). But the more common and standard pattern for these words is *so* + Adj + *that* + statement, e.g., *I am so glad that you came,* and *such* + noun phrase + *that* + statement, e.g., *It was such a good dinner that I hated to stop eating.*

When the teacher reads this story, he will stop and call on you to finish the sentences which use these patterns. Repeat the whole sentence so that you will get a feeling for the way these patterns fit together.

Example:

Teacher: John and James decided to go to the city on Saturday because John wanted to look for a new summer suit. The train was so expensive that . . .

Student: The train was so expensive that they decided to take the bus.

a. It was such a good day that . . .
b. The bus left at 7:30. It was so crowded that . . .
c. The boys could not sit together. John sat by a man who was so fat that . . .
d. James sat by a woman who wanted to talk. She was such a bother that . . .
e. The bus made so much noise that . . .
f. At last they arrived in the city. The bus station was such a crowded place that . . .
g. They couldn't decide which of the many stores they should go to. They asked a man in the station, but he talked so fast that . . .
h. Then they asked a policeman who gave them such clear directions that . . .
i. It was such a long way that . . .
j. They passed a driver who was very reckless. He was so reckless that . . .
k. At last they were at the store where they saw a good-looking suit. It was such a good-looking suit that . . .

l. But the suit was so expensive that . . .
m. Finally the clerk brought out a blue suit that John liked. It was so reasonable in price that . . .
n. John liked the suit so much that . . .
o. After finishing their shopping, the boys went to look for a restaurant where they could eat lunch. They found a good Mexican restaurant and they ordered a big meal. The food was so good that . . .
p. John ate and ate. He ate so much that . . .

Exercise 2. *So . . . that* and *such . . . that* used in complaints:

The teacher will describe an unpleasant situation. Make a complaint about it using either *so . . . that* or *such . . . that.*

Example:

Teacher:	You are in a slow elevator and you want to go to the thirtieth floor.
Student A:	This elevator is moving so slowly that we will never get to the thirtieth floor.
Teacher:	The elevator is crowded.
Student B:	The elevator is so crowded that I can't move.
Teacher:	There is a lot of cigarette smoke.
Student C:	There is such a lot of smoke that I am getting a headache.
Teacher:	A fat man is crowding you.
Student D:	This man is so fat that he is pushing me against the wall.
Teacher:	One man is talking in a very loud voice.
Student E:	He is talking in such a loud voice that I can't think.

a. You are in a terrible prison. Everything about this place is bad.
   The food is poor.
   There is only a little food.
   There are few recreational activities.
   The cells are crowded.
   The cells are dirty.
   The guards are cruel.
   The work is hard.
   The working hours are long.
   You are unhappy.
   All of the prisoners are bored.
b. You are at a sale in a large department store. You have chosen the things that you want and have been waiting twenty minutes for a clerk to help you.
   The store is crowded.

It is very hot.
There are many people to be helped.
There are only a few clerks.
The clerks are tired.
Some of the customers are impatient.
A few of the customers are impolite.
One of the customers is a very rude man.
The clerks are working slowly.
You are tired of waiting.

c. It is 1860. You are riding in a covered wagon across the United States to California.
The horses are moving slowly.
One of your companions is a very sick man.
It's a very hot day.
The desert is dry.
The road is rough.
There is little water.
There is little food.
The wagon is noisy.

d. You invited friends to an expensive restaurant. Everything about your dinner party went wrong.
The soup was salty.
You were served tough steaks.
The coffee was cold.
The waiter was a careless man.
The waiter spoke in a rude manner.
The bill was extremely high.
The party was a complete failure.

Exercise 3. *So . . . that* and *such . . . that* used in compliments:

This time the teacher will describe a different kind of situation. Make up a sentence about the good aspects of the situation. Again use *so . . . that* or *such . . . that.* Be sure to use both patterns. Because it seems a little easier to use *so* with an adjective, than *such* with a noun phrase, perhaps your teacher will specify which one he wants you to use.

Example:

Teacher: Your great-aunt has just died at the age of 100. She has left you and several other people large sums of money. She had always been a generous person.

Student: She was so kind that I loved her even when I was little.

Teacher: She had spent very little money for her own pleasure.

Student: She was such an economical person that I will feel guilty spending her money.
Teacher: She had wanted very much to help others.
Student: She was so helpful that she had many friends.

a. You are staying in a fine hotel at a mountain resort.
The service at the hotel is very good.
The service is prompt.
The meals are delicious.
There is a beautiful lake.
You have friendly companions.
The manager is a considerate person.
Your room is large and comfortable.
The maid cleans the room carefully.

b. You attended an excellent concert. The orchestra played a symphony, and a pianist performed a concerto with the orchestra.
The concert began promptly.
The program had a lot of variety.
The conductor interpreted the symphony well.
The soloist played the concerto beautifully.
The audience was impressed.
You were pleased.
The newspapers wrote excellent reviews.

c. You have just bought a car. Everything about the car pleases you.
The car rides smoothly.
The seats are comfortable.
The car uses very little gas.
The brakes work well.

Lesson Twenty-four

TAG QUESTIONS AND NEGATIVE QUESTIONS

Exercise 1. Agreement of pronouns and verbs in tag questions:

A common way of asking questions is to make a statement and then at the end to add what's called a tag question which usually consists of a verb and a pronoun, e.g., *didn't he?*, *won't they?*, *isn't it?*, etc. If the speaker thinks that the answer to his question will be "yes," then he will probably use falling intonation. If he doesn't know what answer to expect, then he uses rising intonation.

In this exercise the teacher will make the statement. You repeat it and add the tag question. You will have to be careful to use an appropriate pronoun and verb. Whoever answers the questions should answer with a complete sentence instead of just *yes* or *no*, so that he gets more practice.

Examples:

Teacher: A horse flies.
Student A: A horse flies, doesn't it?
Student B: No, a horse doesn't fly.

Teacher: Theodore Roosevelt was the youngest President we have ever had.
Student A: Theodore Roosevelt was the youngest President we have ever had, wasn't he?
Student B: Yes, he was.

a. California is an eastern state.
b. Horses eat grass.
c. Lions are found in Africa.
d. Tan is a common color.
e. The theory of relativity has always been known as Einstein's theory.
f. Three times three is nine.
g. February is the shortest month of the year.
h. July and August are usually very warm in the United States.
i. Switzerland is on the continent of Europe.
j. We have all read in the newspaper about the United Nations.

Exercise 2. Negative Questions:

A negative question differs from a regular question in the assumption underlying it. When a person asks a question posed in the negative, he is indicating that he thinks the answer will be *yes.*

The teacher will ask a question in the usual question pattern. Turn it into the negative pattern. The student who answers it should respond with either *yes* or *no*, plus a statement. In deciding how to answer this kind of question, answer it just as if it did not include *not.*

Example:

Teacher: Is silicosis a disease of the legs?
Student A: Isn't silicosis a disease of the legs?
Student B: No, it is a disease of the lungs.

a. Was George Washington the first President of the United States?
b. Will next year be an election year?
c. Does everyone know that Columbus discovered America?
d. Is the Empire State Building the tallest building in New York City?
e. Were Julius Caesar and Marc Antony Romans?
f. Did Napoleon have two wives?
g. Has it been warm this summer?
h. Will it probably be cold next winter?
i. Do all boys like to play baseball?
j. Was Michelangelo a famous musician?

Exercise 3. Tag questions contrasted with negative questions:

The teacher will ask a question formulated in the negative. Change his question so that you are asking for the same information, only using a tag question. Again, the student who answers should answer in a complete sentence. If the answer is negative, he should give the correct information.

Examples:

Teacher: Didn't Dante write the Divine Comedy?
Student A: Dante wrote the Divine Comedy, didn't he?
Student B: Yes, he did.

Teacher: Isn't a potato a fruit?
Student B: A potato isn't a fruit, is it?
Student C: No, it isn't. It's a vegetable.

Teacher: Shouldn't you have an umbrella when you walk in the rain?

Student C: You should have an umbrella when you walk in the rain, shouldn't you?
Student: Yes, you should. (At least your mother would think so.)

a. Wasn't Beethoven an astronomer?
b. Didn't Edison work in the field of applied science?
c. Didn't Shakespeare write *Hamlet?*
d. Didn't Beethoven compose symphonies?
e. Isn't the Spanish language spoken in Brazil?
f. Wasn't the sky cloudy yesterday?
g. Don't United States citizens have to pay a lot of taxes?
h. Shouldn't children always obey their parents?
i. Wasn't President Roosevelt assassinated?
j. Hasn't Rhode Island always been the smallest state in the Union?
k. Isn't Texas the largest of all the states?

Exercise 4. Tag questions in conversation:

The teacher will describe a situation and a person. Pretend that you are in need of help and you are looking for someone who will be able to assist you. Make up a statement showing what you think that person can help you with. Add a tag question at the end of it. Two or three of you can make up questions about the same situation.

Example:
Teacher: Pretend that you are at the information desk at a large airport. What might you say to the clerk?
Student A: You can show me where to check my luggage, can't you?
Student B: You will check my ticket, won't you?
Student C: You know whether or not the plane is late, don't you?

a. You have just entered the administration building at a large university. You want to apply for admission as a student. You see a secretary at a desk near the door.
b. You have just arrived at the railroad station in a large city where you have never been before. You were to be met by a foreign student advisor. You see a man who looks as if he is watching for someone.
c. You are considering buying a new car. The salesman is very friendly and you are wondering if he will show you how to drive it.

d. One of your teachers has sent you to get a book from the Undergraduate Library. You have never been to that library before, but you find a building which you think is it. A girl smiles at you as she comes out of the front door.

e. You have decided to learn Chinese. Someone tells you that a man named Mr. Wong teaches Chinese in Room 213. You find Room 212, but the room next to it has no number on the door. An oriental man is standing near the desk.

Lesson Twenty-five

PRONOUNS WITH -*Self* OR -*Selves*

Exercise 1. Use of *himself, herself, itself, themselves, yourself, yourselves, myself,* and *ourselves.*

The teacher will make a statement which omits one of the above words. Repeat his statement, putting in the appropriate word. Usually it comes at the end of the sentence.

Examples:

Teacher: He doesn't know __________ .
Student: He doesn't know himself.

Teacher: Take this candy and divide it among __________ .
Student: Take this candy and divide it among yourselves.

a. I can't decide __________ .
b. Be careful; don't hurt __________ .
c. Mary doesn't take very good care of __________ .
d. Did John save any for __________ ?
e. There are some people who should take a good look at __________ .
f. Don't give me all of it; save some for __________ .
g. Why don't you do it __________ ?
h. As members of this class we should tidy up this room __________ .
i. In the summer, the chickens find enough to feed __________ .
j. I thought it was funny that he wrote letters to __________ .
k. I don't want any for __________ .
l. We should do it __________ .
m. I see __________ in the mirror.
n. I read in the newspaper about an elephant that made __________ sick by eating ladies' purses.
o. Please Mother! I would rather do it __________ .

Exercise 2. -*Self* words in context:

Notice the -*self* words in this story which your teacher will read.

A NARROW ESCAPE FOR MR. VICK

Many unsympathetic people laugh to *themselves* about Mr. Vick because he makes many funny mistakes. Mr. Vick, on the other hand, takes *himself* very seriously. He takes pride in *himself* and in his activities. He is also a very cautious man, as you will see for *yourselves.*

The other day, he came home from work early. He felt terrible and called his servant frantically. The servant ran into the room and took one look at his master.

"Mr. Vick, Sir! You should see *yourself!* Just look at *yourself* in the mirror!"

Mr. Vick looked at *himself* in the mirror. He was stunned and thought, "I'm surely dying. I'm bent over almost double. I can't stand up straight. What is the matter? Why can't I straighten *myself* up?"

"Shall I call the doctor?" the servant asked.

"No. I'll call him *myself.* I want to be sure that he comes immediately." Vick called the doctor. Then he started to lie down.

"Shall I take off your shoes or can you take them off *yourself?*"

"Will you do it for me?" groaned Vick. "I can't do it by *myself.* Oh! Such pain!"

The doctor arrived and inspected Vick carefully. Then he began to chuckle to *himself.*

"What's the matter with me?" cried Vick. "Am I dying?"

"No," laughed the doctor. "It's nothing you can't fix *yourself.* You can't straighten *yourself* up because you have fastened the top button of your trousers to the middle buttonhole of your vest!"

In answering the teacher's questions, try to use words with *-self* or *-selves* where they would be appropriate.

Example:

Teacher: What do many unsympathetic people do when they think about Mr. Vick?

Student: They chuckle to themselves.

a. Try to use the phrase "on the other hand" in a sentence about Mr. Vick.
b. Use the phrase "takes pride" in a sentence.
c. How does Mr. Vick think of himself?
d. Did he call his servant in a calm and collected manner? How would you have acted?
e. What did the servant do when he came into the room?
f. When did Mr. Vick get his biggest shock?
g. Did Mr. Vick let the servant call the doctor?
h. What happened when the doctor arrived?
i. What did the servant tell Mr. Vick to do?
j. What did Mr. Vick think to himself?
k. Why did the servant take off Mr. Vick's shoes?
l. What did the doctor say after the examination?

Exercise 3. More practice with *-self* and *-selves:*

Take the different parts of the people in the story and repeat their conversations. You needn't say them exactly as they were in the story. You might even add parts to them. If you happen to have some good actors in your class, it would be fun for three of them to act out the story for the rest of you.

Lesson Twenty-six

Verb + (Verb)-ing CONTRASTED WITH *Verb + to + Verb*

Exercise 1. There are certain verbs in English which can be used with other verbs in either a pattern of *verb + (verb)-ing,* or *verb + to + verb.* In this exercise the teacher will name two verbs. Make up a sentence using them. Feel free to change their tense and number. The second verb is the one that will either take the *-ing* ending or the infinitive *to.* Notice how some of the verbs can be used either way, while others must be used in one or the other of the patterns. If you have trouble, your class might test all of these verbs and with the teacher's help, divide them into three groups: those that take *to,* those that take *-ing,* and those that will take either *to* or *-ing.* Then you could practice with each of the groups.

Examples:

Teacher: begin—dream
Student: I begin dreaming as soon as I go to sleep.
or: I began to dream about my house last night.

Teacher: want—swim
Student: I want to swim in the college pool before I leave.

Teacher: avoid—work
Student: I know someone who avoids working whenever possible.

a. enjoy—dance
b. love—cook
c. begin—clean
d. hate—wash
e. persuade—work
f. avoid—crash
g. like—read
h. practice—jump
i. expect—travel
j. like—work
k. force—confess
l. hate—scrub
m. begin—rake
n. urge—come
o. start—write
p. finish—decorate
q. plan—attend

r. avoid—work
s. consider—apply
t. help—appreciate

Exercise 2. Verb + (verb)-ing and *verb + to + verb* in context:

Notice the use of the *-ing* verb forms and the *verb + to + verb* patterns in this true account of the life of Thomas Edison.

THOMAS EDISON

In the history of applied science, Thomas Alva Edison stands alone. One thousand two hundred patents are credited to him. A Congressional committee once placed the value of his inventions at $15,599,000. He was a man of tremendous energy and phenomenal intelligence.

Edison was born in Milan, Ohio, on February 11, 1847. He *started to work* when he was twelve years old. He *began working* as a train boy in order to help support himself. Three years later, he *began publishing* a small newspaper for the railroad employees.

At sixteen, he *began to learn* telegraphy by himself. He *kept on studying* telegraphy until he became a capable operator. He *enjoyed experimenting* with the equipment where he worked. He just *couldn't help being* curious about scientific matters. He set up a small laboratory in the baggage car of the train and *failed to pay* attention to the orders of his employers. He frequently *forgot to do* the things he was being paid for and even *neglected to relay* messages. His employers asked him *to stop using* their equipment for such purposes, but he *kept on experimenting* until he was fired one day when one of his experiments caused a big explosion in the baggage car. This episode finished Edison's laboratory as well as his job.

When he was seventeen years old, he invented an automatic telegraph repeater. This was the first of his many inventions. He *continued inventing* useful things the rest of his life.

When he was twenty-two, he sold four patents for $40,000. With this money, he *began to set up* an enormous laboratory in Newark, New Jersey. He was extremely happy with his new laboratory. He worked all day and *kept on working* a good part of every night.

Edison *avoided participating* in social activities because he felt that they were a waste of his time. He never *remembered to keep* his appointments, much to the annoyance of his wife and friends. Edison *continued to live* in this manner until his death in 1931. His life was an illustration of his own formula for success: "Two percent inspiration and ninety-eight percent perspiration."

The teacher will name different things from the essay. Tell him what you can about them. Although it will not be possible in all of the sentences, try to get practice using the *verb + (verb)-ing* and the *verb + to + verb* patterns.

a. 1,200 patents
b. over $15,000,000.
c. 1847
d. what Edison did when he was twelve years old
e. Edison as a train boy
f. a small newspaper
g. telegraphy
h. how Edison became a capable operator
i. what he enjoyed doing with the equipment where he worked
j. how he paid attention to his employer's orders
k. how he did the things he was being paid for
l. whether or not he relayed messages
m. what his employers told him
n. what he kept on doing until he was fired
o. his small laboratory
p. a big explosion
q. an automatic telegraph repeater
r. $40,000
s. useful things
t. an enormous laboratory
u. what made Edison extremely happy
v. a good part of every night
w. what he considered a waste of his time
x. what he did much to the annoyance of his wife
y. what he continued to do until his death in 1931
z. his formula for success

Now ask one of your classmates about something in the essay. Either use the teacher's phrase, or make up a question related to it. In both the questions and the answers, try to practice the patterns which you have been concentrating on in this lesson. However, where it is awkward, feel free to use other patterns.

Example:

Teacher: twelve years old
Student A: What did Edison begin doing when he was twelve years old?
Student B: When Edison was twelve, he began working as a train boy.

a. helped support himself
b. a small newspaper
c. at the age of sixteen
d. a capable operator

e. the equipment where he worked
f. his employers
g. until he was fired
h. scientific matters
i. in the baggage car
j. the duties he was being paid for
k. messages
l. a big explosion
m. when he was seventeen
n. an automatic telegraph repeater
o. when he was twenty-two
p. helped him set up an enormous laboratory
q. felt extremely happy
r. felt they were a waste of time
s. his appointments
t. the rest of his life

Exercise 3. *Verb + (verb)-ing* and *verb + to + verb* in conversation:

The teacher will suggest a subject and ask a rather general question about it. When you answer him be as specific as you can. He will be trying to lead you to use the two patterns which you have been practicing. If you cannot fit these patterns in, then use one of the other patterns that you have studied in this book.

Example:
Teacher: Let's talk about Chopin and his work. What did he enjoy?
Student: He enjoyed composing piano music.
Teacher: Why did he like it?
Student: I suppose that he liked to compose piano music because the piano was his favorite instrument.

a. Now tell me about gardeners. What do they usually enjoy?
Do you know what they begin in the spring?
What do they try to do during a dry summer?
b. And careful drivers. What would you say they avoid?
If you were a careful driver, what would you try to do?
What is it that careful drivers never consider?
c. What would you say that good citizens usually insist on?
When can they start voting?
How do they avoid trouble?
d. What did George Frederick Handel want to do when he was a little boy?
Was he able to?
What had his father wanted?
Did his uncle help his father?

e. I am sure you all know some boring people. What do they enjoy?
   How long do they usually keep on?
   Do you think they will never get through?
   What do they always seem to want?
f. A good mechanic is hard to find. When you have one, what do you try?
   What do you avoid?
   What does he often insist on?
g. Poor mechanics are plentiful. Can you always avoid them?
   What can you expect after you have had one?
   If there is something the matter with your car, can a poor mechanic help you?
h. We have all seen impolite dinner guests at parties. When do they usually start their dinner?
   How do they usually finish?
   What do they never consider?
   When they go home, what do they always neglect?
   What do you think the hostess should do?
   What is it that such people need?
i. Do you know what your parents enjoy?
   What is it that they avoid?
   What do all good parents hope?
j. Don't we read in the newspapers that meetings of United Nations delegates continue?
   What is it that they keep trying?
   How long do you think they will keep on?
   When do you think they will get through?
k. There are thieves, unfortunately, in every country. Why do they keep on?
   Why should they not continue?
   When do you think the police can relax and stop arresting people?
   Because of thieves, what is it that we can't help?
l. You have often had good teachers during your school years. Do you think they enjoyed teaching?
   What did they seldom neglect?
   Did you have any teachers who preferred something else?
   Would you say that a good teacher avoids or enjoys talking to good students?
   Why does the teacher you have today keep on teaching?